For
All Catholic Priests
Your angelic ministries bring Christ to us – thank you.

It is truly right and just, our duty and our salvation,
Always and everywhere to give you thanks,
Lord, holy Father, almighty and eternal God,
And to praise you without end
In your Archangels and Angels.
For the honor we pay the angelic creatures
In whom you delight
Redounds to your own surpassing glory,
And by their great dignity and splendor
You show how infinitely great you are,
To be exalted above all things,
Through Christ our Lord.
Through him the multitude of angels extols your majesty,
And we are united with them in exultant adoration
As with one voice we acclaim:
Holy, Holy, Holy, Lord God of Hosts,
Heaven and earth are full of your glory,
Hosanna in the highest!
Blessed is he who comes in the name of the Lord,
Hosanna in the highest!

(Preface for the Votive Mass of the Holy
Angels, *Roman Missal*, 3rd Edition, 2012.)

CONTENTS

Introduction: Holy Card Angels 9

    Chapter 1: Angel Ministries 15

    Chapter 2: Christian Myths about Angels 25

    Chapter 3: Non-Christian Myths about Angels 35

    Chapter 4: Truths about Angels in Themselves 45

    Chapter 5: Truths about Angels in Relation to Us 55

    Chapter 6: Angelic Organizations 67

    Chapter 7: Angelic Religious Orders 79

    Chapter 8: Awesome Angels 89

    Chapter 9: Avenging Angels 99

    Chapter 10: Artists, Rescue Our Angels! 109

    Chapter 11: Accurate Angel Art 121

Conclusion: Praying to Angels 129

    Appendix 1: Fire and Ice 135

    Appendix 2: The Nine Choirs of Angels 139

    Appendix 3: Prayer for an Angelic Heart 143

Bibliography 145

Acknowledgments 151

About the Author 153

"Bless the LORD, all you his angels, mighty in strength, acting at his behest, obedient to his command."

PSALM 103:20

Introduction

HOLY CARD ANGELS

If you've ever seen a holy card of a guardian angel, it's probably one that features a large, feminine, winged being in a flowing gown with a star above her head hovering next to a couple of little kids as they cross a rickety bridge over a raging stream. She's making sure they don't fall in the water.

Isn't that sweet.

Actually, no. It's the worst possible depiction of an angel for at least three reasons:

1. Angels aren't female.
2. Guardian angels don't hover around you.
3. A guardian angel's primary job is not to keep you from drowning.

While I'm at it, let me add a fourth. You know those fluffy angel wings everybody likes? No guardian angel has them.

Shocked? Good.

My mission is to purge all those pietistic and awful cultural angel images from your mind because real angels – God's magnificent servants – aren't like that. They're more like incandescent fire, and we all know we shouldn't play with fire.

Angels are awesome in every respect. They are awe-inspiring and *awe-full* in the traditional meaning of filling you with wonder about things greater than and beyond you.

NATURES OF FIRE

Angels are so vastly powerful, intelligent, and full of life that there is nothing on earth even remotely like them. We should never attempt to reduce them to comfortable versions of ourselves. They're not the stuff of holy cards.

They are *manifestations of the holiness of God* that comes to meet us in the circumstances of our real lives.

The prophet Daniel had some insight into this: "His throne was flames of fire," Daniel said, "with wheels of burning fire. A river of fire surged forth, flowing from where he sat; thousands upon thousands were ministering to him, and myriads upon myriads stood before him" (Dan 7:9-10).

Those thousands and myriads ministering to God are angels, and they seem to be immersed in that "river of fire", a metaphor for God's holiness.

To understand invisible things we have to use analogies to visible things, even though analogies always fall short of the reality. In the case of the angelic nature, physical fire serves as a fitting metaphor.

Fire symbolizes many human dynamics: we can burn with love, be on fire with passion, radiate goodness, or glow with zeal. We can "catch fire" or "get fired up" or "burn with intensity" at anything that enthuses us. Fire cleanses fields of chaff and purges impurities from metal. All of these images are rich with spiritual overtones pointing out some of the capacities of the angelic nature.

Of course, fire can also burn your house down. Wildfires rage out of control in destructive rampages. Metaphorically, you can "scorch" someone with criticism or "set fire" to someone's reputation.

The destructive aspect of fire is also a metaphor for the flames of hell that can encompass you through the power of sin and evil. Angels are sent to protect us from that too because God fights fire with fire.

SUPERNATURAL FIRE

Have you ever considered how many times scripture associates angels with fire? It's more than a casual connection if we consider the number of references in question. Here are ten of them from Genesis to Revelation, and there are at least a dozen more:[1]

- The angel that stood guard over Eden held a fiery sword (Gen 3:24)
- Two angels destroyed Sodom and Gomorrah with fire and brimstone (Gen 19:24)
- An angel appeared as a "pillar of fire" to protect the Israelites (Ex 13:21; 40:38)
- Elisha opened the eyes of his servant to see thousands of angels on the hillsides in the form of horses and chariots of fire (2 Kgs 6:17)
- A seraph purged Isaiah's prophetic lips with fire (Is 6:7)
- "Flashing fire" came out of Ezekiel's Cherubim (Ez 1:4)
- An angel stands in the fiery furnace with the three young men (Dn 3:25)
- Angels will be dispatched at the end of time to throw the wicked into the eternal flames (Mt 13:40.50)
- An angel of the Resurrection appears as a bolt of lightning over the tomb of Christ (Mt 28:2)
- An angel is in charge of the fire of the altar of incense in heaven (Rev 8:5).

The holy angels are associated with fire as a symbol of their identities, but they are not warm and cuddly creatures as we understand

---

1. For example: Ex 2:23ff; Num 21:6; Jdg 6:21 and 13:20; 2 Kgs 2:11; Ps 104:4; Ez 1:14; Dan 7:10; Mt 25:41; Lk 10:18; Heb 1:7; Rev 20:1; Rev 20:10.

emotional warmth. They are *perfectly good creatures* as we understand the spiritual warmth of the saintly personality.

Angels bear that fire of God's holiness to the world, sometimes in dramatic ways. We see the most obvious example of it in the story of Moses's calling. Moses is captivated by a fascinating sight, which is described as something more than a burning bush. It is a fiery angel: "The angel of the LORD appeared to him as fire flaming out of a bush. When he looked, although the bush was on fire, it was not being consumed" (Ex 3:2).

From there, the LORD Himself takes over: "God said: Do not come near! Remove your sandals from your feet, for the place where you stand is holy ground" (Ex 3:5). The angel has done his job. He bore the supernatural fire to Moses and initiated the dialogue and encounter with God. The angel brought sanctification, even to the earth itself, which he consecrated by his presence in the vanguard of God's appearance.

In many biblical passages, it is difficult to distinguish the angel messenger from the LORD in any given encounter. Numerous stories in the Old Testament refer to the "angel of the LORD" who speaks with the voice of God Himself or who initiates encounters, such as in the account of the burning bush, then promptly disappears and God continues.[2] That is a privilege of the angelic mission as divine emissary and a sign of how perfectly one the angel is with his LORD.

SERVANTS OF THE ORIGINAL FIRE

Yet, we must keep the *infinite difference* between the divine nature and the created angelic nature very much in mind as we read. Angels are worthy of admiration and respect in every sense, but they are not God, not divine entities, not supernatural[3] personas or demi-gods. If angels are natures of fire, it is because they are servants of the original, supernatural fire "from which all fire is born," says English writer Judith Lang.[4]

---

2. When Abraham meets three angels in Genesis 18, they are presented as "the Lord" himself, a reference the Fathers of the Church all considered to be a symbol and foretaste of the Trinity.
3. I explain why angels are not "supernatural" beings in Chapter 2.
4. Judith Lang, *The Angels of God: Understanding the Bible* (New York: New City Press, 1997), 125.

Nor must we ever presume that God *needs* angels in any way to accomplish His purposes. Everything the angels do, God could easily accomplish by divine decree. When He chooses to send them as His representatives, it is because He loves them and has given them some clear purpose in His Kingdom. God bestows His holiness on all His creatures in ways befitting their natures, just as Christ gave His Church the great commission to evangelize the world.

In this book I've lit a dozen or so spiritual flames for you in the form of short chapters to help you come to know more about the angelic nature. I hope this book opens your mind to a profound sense of wonderment at God's magnificent servants and that your journey to understanding them will be full of the light and warmth of the spiritual fire holy angels bring to the world.

This angel fire can totally transform your spiritual life and set you aflame with zeal and virtue. That fire will put you more firmly on the path to heaven, if you let it.

Angels do that. *That's* their job.

1

ANGEL MINISTRIES

If I've given the impression thus far that angels are kind of standoffish in their heavenly splendor, nothing could be further from the truth. Angels *do* a great deal for us in real time, here on earth, and on a regular basis. It's just that most of what they do is behind the scenes.

Remember the traditional Guardian Angel Prayer you were taught as a child?

> *Angel of God, my guardian dear,*
> *To whom God's love commits me here;*
> *Ever this day, be at my side,*
> *To light and guard, to rule and guide.*
> *Amen.*

Such a wonderful prayer! Angels minister to us invisibly by lighting, guarding, ruling, and guiding, among other things. They're our mentors and servants of our souls even though we rarely notice their presence. Judith Lang speaks very perceptively of the angelic vocation to serve us:

> The relation of the human soul to its own guardian angel is closer and more intense than any other mode of relation within the created universe. The birth, death and

resurrection of Christ reveal that God's highest intention is to bring the whole human race into himself through Christ. Guardian angels have this single task and their power is directly the power of salvation in Christ.... That soul is their life, in relation to God.[5]

In other words, the angel that God assigns to each one of us is entirely focused on the work of *our* salvation. If only *we* were so focused!

MENTORS AND GUIDES

An analogy might be the best way to explain their ministries. Imagine having your favorite teacher available to you 24/7/365. (Okay, from a human point of view that would get kind of annoying, but stay with me.)

The teacher is there to assist you with your ongoing education about life. You can ask a question about anything, and he'll give you a perfect answer. You can ask for favors and assistance, and he will help you. You can ask him to open up avenues for advancement, and the doors will just fly open for you. He also keeps you from going down the wrong career path and advises you against relationships and activities that will harm you. Even better, your teacher really likes you and has no other purpose than to help you learn and get ahead in life. What an amazing resource that would be.

But then you ignore him. "I got this," you say and go off on your merry way. This is the manner in which many people treat their guardian angels.

In fact, many of us bounce between two tendencies: either ignoring our angels or having infantile views of them. The truth of angels is that they are immensely powerful spiritual resources for our lives, and the better we understand their ministries to us, the more we benefit.

So, if angels are not our personal butlers or domestic helpers, what do they actually do for us? Here are seven standard ways the holy guardian angels assist us in our spiritual journey.

---

5   Judith Lang, *The Angels of God: Understanding the Bible* (NY: New City Press, 1997), 166.

1. Revealing

Angels have a complete understanding of the natural world[6] and a perfect grasp of all the truths of the faith. In a 2011 article in *Crisis* magazine,[7] Marquette University professor Howard Kainz used the following computer analogy to explain angelic knowledge: angels have a full hard drive of information about the world, which God installed in them at the moment of their creation. In other words, angels know literally *everything* there is to know about the natural world either directly or potentially.

To extend the computer analogy, they have an "operating system" (their active intellects) that accesses any information they need to fulfill their missions. They're not omniscient like God, but they can "call up" relevant information instantaneously when needed. In other words, never try to match wits with an angel. You're doomed to fail. (We'll deal more with angelic minds in Chapter 4.)

Because of that capacity, angels teach us by *revealing* both natural and spiritual knowledge to us; they open our minds to a deeper understanding of the structure of reality or to "see" things that may be essential for our lives and vocations.

In scripture, for example, the Archangel Gabriel several times reveals knowledge of the divine plan to others (Daniel, Zechariah, the Virgin Mary, John of Revelation). This dynamic also accounts for the numerous stories of angels who reveal future pregnancies (to the mothers of Samuel and Samson, 1 Sam 1, Jdg 13) and above all to Our Lady (Lk 1:26-38).

Angels bless and assist those who honestly wish to know the truth. They enlighten those who study the scriptures and open our hearts to new insights. Angels can make us see things we've been blind to or communicate information that leads to our conversion of heart. But they can only help us if we, like Daniel, "make up our minds" (Dan 10:12) to live according to the truth.

---

6 Mortimer J. Adler, *The Angels and Us* (New York: MacMillan Publishing Company, Inc., 1982), 135; Mark Miravalle, *Time to Meet the Angels: The Nine Choirs and Much More* (Homer Glen: Gabriel Press, 2013), 12.

7 Howard Kainz, *Crisis*, "Artificial Intelligence and Angelology", November 28, 2011.

2. Teaching Reverence

In the Book of Revelation, John made the mistake of falling down to worship an angel (Rev 19:10), but the angel rebuked him for his error. Angels do not want us to worship them. They worship God alone and teach us how to adore God more perfectly.

Reverence (also called piety) is an essential virtue of the Christian life, a gift of the Holy Spirit. The angel who rebuked John was not being humble. He was simply insisting on the proper order of reverence given by God in the First Commandment, "You shall not have other gods beside me...you shall not bow down before them or serve them" (Ex 20:3.5). He taught John to overcome the feeling of awe that people often have in the presence of a glorious spiritual being like an angel.

We are not born with that angelic desire to put God first. We must learn it over the course of our lives. Angels help us to overcome our laziness about spiritual things (like when we would rather sleep in on Sunday instead of going to church) and to keep our priorities in proper order. They also assist us in forming the virtue of reverence in others, especially our children.

3. Strengthening

Angels accompany us on the long haul of the spiritual life, which transpires as we strive to overcome the challenges of the world, the flesh, and the devil. Yet, to grow in spiritual strength we must learn to *persevere* in the truth and to desire God's will above all things. Angels develop that spiritual capacity within us.

The prophet Elijah is a good example of this kind of perseverance. He was threatened by the evil queen Jezebel, who wanted to kill him for calling the people of Israel back to fidelity to Yahweh. Driven into exile, Elijah collapsed with weariness from his fight, and God sent an angel to strengthen him. When you have a moment, read the story in 1 Kgs 19:4-8 to see how effectively the angel revived Elijah's strength to carry out his mission.

The human will is capricious. Weaknesses of the flesh, temptations, and spiritual laziness make our desire to serve God unreliable at best.

We often fail to persevere in righteousness. Living a virtuous life is not easy. It takes practice. The angels strengthen our wills to do the right thing, and to do it especially when we would rather not.

4. Opening

The Apostles experienced the door-opening power of an angel more than once. In Acts 16, St. Paul and his companions intended to go to a certain region of Asia Minor (modern day Turkey), but "the Spirit of Jesus did not allow them" (Acts 16:7). That very night St. Paul had a vision of a "man from Macedonia" (northern Greece) who opened a door to the preaching of the Gospel in a region that had never heard of Jesus. Today we have five books of the New Testament (1-2 Corinthians, Philippians, and 1-2 Thessalonians) to show that the angel's ministry bore immense fruit from that single open door into Macedonia.

Angels sometimes get us out of tight fixes too, especially when we're doing the work of the Kingdom. Angels freed the disciples from prison and sent them back to preach the gospel in the Temple area without fear (Acts 5:17-21). St. Peter's own guardian angel helped him escape from jail when Herod wanted to kill him (Acts 12:6-11). In the latter incident, the iron locks and doors of the prison immediately fell away at the command of the angel. Human and material barriers are worthless when an angel is sent to open a door.

We don't have to be missionaries to receive an angel's help. They open doors for anyone who does God's will and work.

5. Boundary-setting

Angels carry out that same "blocking" function that Paul experienced in Asia Minor. They set limits to human sinfulness and even to well-intentioned designs that are not in accord with God's will.

We see the clearest example of an angel barrier in the humorous story of Balaam and the talking donkey in the Book of Numbers. Balaam, some kind of pagan seer, was commissioned by an enemy of Israel to place a curse on God's people, but the LORD sent an angel to block his way (Num 22:22-23).

Evidently, the donkey on which he was riding was more perceptive to spiritual things than the seer (which is what makes the scene so funny). The beast *spoke* to Balaam[8] and told him an angel was standing right in front of him! The story concluded happily with Balaam pronouncing a blessing over Israel instead of a curse. We can never be as perceptive about God's will as angels are, so they may, from time to time, step in to make us change course.

We must discern these blockages carefully. As just noted, sometimes it is the Spirit of Jesus or His angel who blocks us. At other times it is the devil who tries to prevent us from carrying out God's purposes.

Whenever the source of a blockage is unclear, we should be patient and ask our guardian angels to clarify God's will for us before rushing into action. Angels are guides on our journey to heaven and sometimes stop us when we want to do something we shouldn't.

6. Amplifying Prayer

The Book of Tobit is clearly the most extraordinary angelophany (angel appearance) in the bible.[9] What makes the story of Tobit so intriguing is the presence of the Archangel Raphael, who plays a decisive role in the lives of Tobit and his family throughout the book.

Chief among Raphael's many abilities is his readiness to answer prayers in a huge way. He is the emissary of God's will, a point he is careful to emphasize: "Now when you, Tobit, and Sarah prayed, it was I who presented the record of your prayer before the Glory of the LORD" (Tob 12:12).

In the depths of Tobit's and Sarah's agonizing hearts were hidden genuine prayers, not just for their own welfare but also for the good of others. The angel knew the full extent of their unspoken prayers. By the end of the book, Raphael had succeeded in healing Tobit's blindness, freeing Sarah from the grip of a demon, marrying her to Tobias, and recovering a lost family fortune in gold!

---

8   Except for the serpent in Genesis (which is really an angel taking on physical form), this is the only example in scripture of an animal talking.

9   Pascal P. Parente, *The Angels: The Catholic Teaching of the Angels* (Rockford: TAN Books, 1994), 93.

Angels are *amplifiers* of prayer because the answers they bring often go far beyond what people actually pray for. In a sense, angelic power can transform the prayer from its self-centered character to a spiritually pure petition before God.

God hears each and every prayer we offer, especially prayers born of suffering and anguish. He sees the depths of the heart and sends His holy angels to minister to the needs of the faithful. Angels have power to multiply the effects of our prayers, even when we are not aware of what we really need.

7. Purifying

Isaiah's vision of the Seraphim in the Temple is the greatest example of angelic purification found in scripture. In the vision, God sends an angel to brand the prophet's lips with an ember from the heavenly altar. "Now that this has touched your lips," says the angel, "your wickedness is removed, your sin purged" (Is 6:1-7).

The amazing story of Isaiah's encounter with the highest of all angels is worth reading many times over. Angels, being completely pure, have a powerful ability to purify our souls and make them ready for heaven or for the mission God entrusts to us.

That is probably why angels are often associated with fire in scripture, as I noted in the Introduction. In fact, the Greek word for fire is *puros* (πύρος), the root of the English words "pure" and "purify".

We can ask the angels to purify us, but we need the moral courage to accept the purification of our sinfulness, as Isaiah experienced. An angel's capacity to help us is not limited by the angel's nature, it is limited by ours.

To the extent that we invest ourselves in our own spiritual development, our angel's ability to help us increases. If we neglect our spiritual lives, the angels can do very little for us. They are bound by God's iron law of free will and cannot force their help on us. Only we can change our own hearts.

MINISTRIES OF DEMONS

Some of the Fathers of the Church believed that the devil assigns a guardian demon to souls just as God assigns a guardian angel.[10] That point of view has never been endorsed officially in any Church doctrine, but it does signal a fundamental aspect of the mission of the *fallen* angels: they are set against man's salvation as a matter of principle and obsessive desire.

The fallen angels have their own ministries that are the polar opposites of the angelic ministries. They are the terrorists of the spiritual world:

1. Whereas the holy angels *reveal*, the fallen angels obscure the truth, lie, darken the intellect, and cause confusion and chaos.

2. Whereas the holy angels *teach reverence*, the fallen angels teach blasphemy, impiety, disregard for the sacred, and mockery and defamation of holiness.

3. Whereas the holy angels *strengthen spiritually*, the fallen angels lead into sin, weaken wills, and justify violations of God's commandments.

4. Whereas the holy angels *open*, the fallen angels close off pathways to holiness, harden hearts, and steal the stirrings of grace in our souls like the birds in the Parable of the Sower (Mt 13:1-23) that eat the seeds that fall on the pathway.

5. Whereas the holy angels *set healthy spiritual and moral boundaries*, the fallen angels break down barriers to sin and error.

6. Whereas the holy angels *amplify prayer*, the fallen angels derail attention we are supposed to give to the things of God, and suppress spiritual and holy desires.

---

10 Jean Danielou, S.J., Christian Classics Series, tr. David Heimann, *The Angels and Their Mission* (Notre Dame, Indiana: Ave Maria Press, 1957), 71.79-82. In fact, this ancient tradition is the origin of the popular image of an angel on one shoulder and a demon on the other, both whispering in your ear.

7. Whereas the holy angels *purify*, the fallen angels sully souls, lead them into moral compromise, and confirm them in sin.

Combining all the works of the holy angels into a single ministry is rather simple: their entire job is to get us to heaven and share eternal life with God. The work of the evil angels is the opposite: to lead us to eternal death.

As many saints have said, the spiritual life is a kind of warfare, and the holy angels are on our side in the battle against these spiritual terrorists. The most sobering reality of all is that none of us would reach heaven without the aid of the holy angels.

The question is whether *we even realize* that we are engaged in mortal combat for our very souls.

2

CHRISTIAN MYTHS ABOUT ANGELS

Why should Christians study angels at all? Boston College philosopher Peter Kreeft says that humans have a natural fascination with intelligent beings in "a non-human form".[11] His idea is that if we love dogs and dolphins and elephants for their innate intelligence, then we should love the angels even more. Their intelligence far surpasses ours.

Angels are, without a doubt, fascinating creatures, but just like animals, they are not mental concepts. Angels are real, holy, powerful, spiritual beings. They are as real as the person sitting across the table from us – but they are invisible. Yet, it can be difficult to grasp the reality of beings we can't see.

Some misunderstandings about angels come from bad catechesis (or lack of catechesis altogether) and others come from the skewed cultural notions about angels that have infiltrated the Christian faith. I'll address that issue further in Chapter 10. For starters, though, let's debunk some pious Christian myths about angels – a few of which may surprise you.

---

11 Peter Kreeft, *Angels (and Demons): What Do We Really Know About Them?* (San Francisco: Ignatius Press, 1995), 20.

1. "ANGELS ARE SUPERNATURAL BEINGS"

One of the most common misconceptions about angels (and demons) is that they are supernatural beings, but angels are not supernatural in a strict sense. Only God is supernatural: the creator of nature and everything that exists. We describe Him with the term *super*-natural because we don't know a better way to say that He is above all things and beyond all human definition.

Technically, angels are *preternatural* beings; the prefix *praeter* comes from the Latin word for "beyond", "apart from", and "over". The word "paranormal" has essentially the same meaning[12] but has been completely co-opted by reality TV in the form of ghost hunting shows and cheap horror flicks, and we should never use it. In their original meanings, these terms simply indicate that angels exist outside our capacity to sense them.

The *Catechism of the Catholic Church* reminds us that angels are created beings – creatures – not gods or God. They are not "extensions" of God's essence, as New Agers and pantheists believe. Angels have their own nature, distinct from the essence of God. Here is how the *Catechism* defines them:

> The angels are purely spiritual creatures, incorporeal, invisible, immortal, and personal beings endowed with intelligence and will. They ceaselessly contemplate God face-to-face and they glorify him. They serve him and are his messengers in the accomplishment of his saving mission to all.[13]

The Church has been very clear on this point from the beginning, as can be seen in both scripture and Church history.

For example, in 1 Corinthians 10:20, St. Paul condemns pagan sacrifices to "gods" (who were really just fallen angels). St. Augustine, likewise, condemned a 3rd century Christian sect in North Africa called the "Angelici" for their practice of worshipping *holy* angels. Whether

---

12 *Praeter* is a Latin prefix; *para* is a Greek prefix. The "normal" world is the world of nature, even if it includes the esoteric world of angels. Angels are still natural creations of God and not supernatural.
13 *Compendium of the Catechism of the Catholic Church* (Città del Vaticano: Libreria Editrice Vaticana, 1995), 60.

the tendency is to worship holy or unholy angels, the Christian faith forbids it. We worship only the one supernatural Being we call God.

2. "ANGELS ARE INVISIBLE INHABITANTS OF OUR WORLD"

Peter Kreeft, in his book *Angels and Demons*, says that "angels don't belong in this universe. (They're visitors.)" He calls them "extraterrestrials".[14]

Kreeft is being clever, but he is also correct in saying that the angels aren't members of our world. This doesn't mean that angels are creatures from another planet either! Even if that were the case, they would still be part of this physical universe. They are not.

Everything that exists in the universe is part of the space-time continuum, even if that continuum is sometimes mysterious to us. We don't understand the vastness of outer space, for example, but *space itself* is part of the vast created universe. Albert Einstein also showed that the concept of time is not a fixed reality, as Sir Isaac Newton taught. Apparently, time is malleable – it can be lengthened or shortened – relative to the speed of light.[15]

Following Einstein, quantum physics has shown how little we know about the elements of the microscopic world, where particles of atoms seem to follow no laws of physics in their movements.[16] The weak human mind has trouble understanding anything as existing outside of the time-space continuum, so let's briefly examine what our human terms "time" and "space" mean with regard to angels.

Time

Angels are part of the created universe, but they are not part of the time-space continuum as we know it. They experience time and space (analogously) in a way that is different from material creation. I've tried to summarize this complex subject in the chart below that shows the relationships of all created realties to time.

---

14 Kreeft, *Angels (and Demons)*, 47. Anyone familiar with Peter Kreeft's writing knows he's being clever to make a theological point.

15 A couple of fascinating modern movies have attempted to illustrate what Einsteinian physics says would happen to people who travel through time (*Captain America*, 2011) or into outer space and back (*Interstellar*, 2014).

16 Thomas Dubay, *The Evidential Power of Beauty: Science and Theology Meet* (San Francisco: Ignatius Press, 1999), 166-168.

CREATURES AND TIME		
Being / Entity	Type of Existence	Type of Time
Physical universe; world of plants and animals[17]	Material; began to exist at their creation and will die or be transformed into "a new heaven and a new earth" (Rev 21) at the end of time.	Chronological
Human beings	Material / spiritual; began to exist at the moment of conception; is both mortal in body and immortal in soul.	Chronological (body) / timeless (soul)
Angels	Purely spiritual; began to exist at God's decree; is immortal by nature.	Aeveternal (see below)

Since God, the Creator, is not a created being, I haven't included Him on this list! We can speak of creatures as immortal, meaning that they were created at one point and will live forever after that, but we can't speak of God as immortal, except analogously. It is best to describe Him as eternal, meaning *uncreated*, with no beginning or end. All things exist *in Him* who is pure being, omniscient, omnipresent, and omnipotent by His very nature.

Here's the specific problem for angels. They are in a sort of time limbo. They don't share human chronological (sequential, linear) time because they don't have material bodies. But they also do not share God's eternity because they are creatures. So where exactly are they on this time spectrum?

Ancient and medieval philosophers said that angels exist somewhere

---

17 Although the Church teaches that animals do not have immortal souls like human beings, it is reasonable to believe that animals will be full-fledged members of the "new heavens and new earth", however that may be constituted. It is not the purpose of an angel book to discuss whether all pets go to heaven!

in the middle distance between the two, an area between chronological time and eternity that they called "aeveternity".[18] (It was those clever medievals who invented the term for this middle reality.) The word itself is also an in-between word composed of the two Latin terms for "time" (*aevus*) and "eternity" (*aeternitas*).

Thus, angels exist in a dimension that can be thought of, paradoxically, as "time-eternity". It is a quasi-time concept that explains how angels can parachute into our world and create change in the ongoing flow of hours and days while also retaining their timeless nature as ministers of the things of heaven.

Can we measure aeveternity? Not exactly, at least not in the same way we measure chronological time. When we speak of angelic time we have to shift from quantitative measurements (seconds, minutes, and hours) to *quasi-time expressions* or analogies to time which designate the experience of an event rather than a measurement of its duration.

In the Book of Daniel, for example, Gabriel tells Daniel that the prince of Persia stood in his way for "twenty-one days" (Dan 10:13). The angel was not describing an exact period of three weeks but a particular event – an angelic struggle – that had a distinct beginning and end in the world of angels. That is angelic time.

Aeveternity also describes the effect of angelic actions in human time. In the Temptation in the Desert, for example, Luke says that the devil (an angel) took Jesus up to a mountain and "showed him all the kingdoms of the world in an instant" (Lk 4:5). An *instant* is another one of those quasi-time designations that has no duration. It's a point, not a line. Angelic acts take place "instantaneously" as if the angel inserts himself into a single second of human time to perform his action and then retreats back into his timeless world.[19]

If you can't quite wrap your mind around how this all works, don't worry, neither can I! The angels' relationship to time is part of their

---

18 Adler, *Angels and Us*, 79.
19 Those who have seen the 2014 "X-Men" movie *Days of Future Past* may remember the dramatic kitchen scene where all action stops and the character Quicksilver runs around the room changing the outcome of events once time resumes again. He is so quick that his actions take place in an "instant" of time. That's Hollywood's version of angelic instantaneous action, and it's actually quite accurate!

mystery and another reason we cannot relate to them in humanly familiar ways. If I ever make it to heaven and meet St. Thomas Aquinas, I intend to have a long talk with him about the aeveternity of angels.[20]

Space

Regarding physical space, here is the key concept to ponder: angels are never "in" space; it's better to say that space is *in them*. That is, they "surround" physical space by their superior ability to be mentally involved in the things happening in any given physical space.

Peter Kreeft uses the analogy of a theatre setting, a stage, to describe this concept. He says that an angel contains (i.e., surrounds) a place with his mind and presence in much the same way that a stage for a play "contains" the actors and the action.[21] It's a nice concept. We can all understand that a stage is larger than and actually *encompasses* the action of a play.

In other words, when angels turn their attention to what is happening in a particular physical place, they are "in" that place spiritually, though they are not a material element of the place as a real-time actor, director, or stage prop. This may be why we can "feel" *the presence* of an angel in a given place, but the angel won't be bound and constricted by that place in the same way humans are.

Now you might also understand why I said in the beginning that angels don't "hover" around people. They don't need to. All they have to do is think about us to be present to us. (The same is true of demons.)

3. "ANGELS CAN READ OUR MINDS"

Since angels are spiritual beings, many people think they can actually read a person's mind. Minds are spiritual, right? The short answer is that angels cannot read our minds, but there is also a long answer that requires a few words of explanation.

In an absolute sense, the human mind and will are closed sanctuaries

---

20 Peter Kreeft probably comes closest to clarifying the concept when he notes that angels act like strobe lights or as neutrons and electrons do in quantum leaps. We will explain this a little further in the next chapter. Kreeft, *Angels (and Demons)*, 69-70, 92.
21 Kreeft, *Angels (and Demons)*, 68-69.

to anyone other than the owner and his Creator. Thank God. Even angels are not allowed entrance to the inner sanctum of these spiritual faculties[22] of the human person. Here's where things get complicated.

The grand exception to this "inner sanctuary" law is that we can voluntarily open our minds and hearts to others, including angels and demons, just as we can open our houses to visitors. We do this when we put ourselves under the guidance of authorities like teachers, counselors, or spiritual directors. We can open ourselves in a similar way to our closest spiritual companions, our own guardian angels.

On the negative side, any fascination with the occult, any dabbling in forbidden practices *opens us up* to the influence of fallen angels. Here we must avoid any overstatement. Demonic spirits generally can't harm us through casual contact with the occult, or by just thinking about them, but the longer we are in contact with occult things, the more likely demons are to gain entry into our thoughts and decisions. The concept of free will applies here too: if we voluntarily open ourselves to occult realities, we give permission to demons to enter our lives and influence us.

There is another dynamic that explains how angels can know our thoughts. People can become "open books" to us if we are in regular, close contact with them. We understand a lot about our intimate friends and family because we spend the most time with them and are familiar with their regular habits, mannerisms, likes and dislikes, etc.

It is precisely by this kind of intuitive knowledge that angels and demons can "read" us, even if we don't directly give them access to our inner faculties. They study us and become very familiar with our standard reactions to things, our attitudes, our common tendencies and prejudices. An angel can forecast what we are *likely* to do or how we will react in any given circumstance with frightening accuracy because of his familiarity with our predictable patterns.

So, the short answer is that, in an absolute sense, angels cannot read our minds unless we give them permission. The long answer is

---

[22] I am taking the traditional view of the human soul as a three-part reality. The two spiritual faculties are mind and will. The flesh-bound part of the human soul is called the memory or imagination (consisting of the senses, emotions, desires, passions, etc.).

that, even without permission, they *can make good guesses about* what we're thinking due to their familiarity with us and their unique powers of perception.

4. "THE DEVIL WILL BE REDEEMED IN THE END"

Speaking of demons, a common theological temptation (pardon the pun) is to want to redeem the devil. A 2nd century theologian named Origen of Alexandria once held that God would eventually turn a blind eye to all rebellion and would forgive the devil, his minions, and all damned human souls at the end of time. The idea is that God is *such a nice guy* that, in the end, He will just wipe out hell and allow everyone to live forever with Him in bliss.

This idea is more commonly called "universal salvation",[23] meaning that everyone will be saved in the end, including the devil. This was the first theology of nice in Church history, but it got poor old Origen officially condemned at the Second Council of Constantinople in 553.[24] (It's one reason why this brilliant theologian is not known as *Saint* Origen of Alexandria today.)

The opposite of this error is that all evil spirits and souls will be annihilated at the end of time, an opinion that was condemned by the Fifth Lateran Council (1512-17). This is an erroneous Jehovah's Witness teaching which endures to this day.[25]

The concept of hell is hard for people to swallow, but hell's existence is a truth of the Christian faith. I subscribe to the opinion of Fr. Dwight Longenecker, who states that the idea of universal salvation is a "demonic trick" that

---

23 The idea never seems to lose popularity. One of the Catholic Church's foremost theologians, Hans Urs von Balthasar, dabbled with the idea in his 1986 book, *Dare We Hope "That All Men be Saved"?* The famous Protestant theologian, David Bentley Hart, also advocated for this idea in his 2019 book called *That All Shall Be Saved: Heaven, Hell, and Universal Salvation*.

24 Parente, *The Angels*, 110-11; Origen also had a few other strange ideas about angels, such as his belief that bad angels could be converted into good angels with the baptism of the person in their charge.

25 Bishop Athanasius Schneider and Diane Montagna, *Christus Vincit: Christ's Triumph Over the Darkness of the Age* (Brooklyn, NY: Angelico Press, 2019), 315.

has lulled thousands into the false security that in the end it doesn't matter what they do and what they choose because they will all make it to heaven at last. Satan loves universalism because he gets to dress up his lie in the clothes of the Father's greatest attribute: the Divine Mercy. The best way to repudiate this lie is to fear hell.[26]

There's no getting around the drastic nature of hell.

One might say that sheer stubbornness is essentially what keeps Satan and his riff-raff from ever being redeemed. St. Thomas Aquinas has a more precise term for it: he calls it "obstinacy of will".[27] Satan and his demons are perfectly obstinate (unrepentant) in their sin, and that obstinacy has an everlasting character corresponding to the immortality of their beings.

Thomas taught that when angels make decisions, they make them with full understanding and with their whole being, not tentatively, like human beings make decisions. This applies particularly to the *first* major decision that angels were given to make, the decision to serve God or not. The fallen angels adamantly rejected the service of God.

The lack of a second chance for the fallen angels has nothing to do with God's capacity to forgive. The reason fallen angels cannot return to heaven at any time is that they *will not*.[28] They were fully aware of the consequences of that decision before they made it and, ever after that decision, they live in an eternal rejection of grace. Even if God were to get down on His metaphorical knees and beg Satan to return to heaven, Satan would still snub the offer with haughty contempt.

We should take care not to be too glib in condemning the wicked angels, however. They got what they deserved, but there will be a

---

26 Fr. Dwight Longenecker, *Patheos*, "Ten Tricks of the Devil to Watch Out For," 1/10/16, http://www.patheos.com/blogs/standingonmyhead/2016/01/ten-tricks-of-the-devil-to-watch-out-for.html, accessed 1/11/16.

27 Aquinas, *Summa*, I.64.2.

28 A reference to the defiant proclamation of satanic disobedience is found in Jer 2:20, "Long ago you broke your yoke, you tore off your bonds. You said, 'I will not serve.' On every high hill, under every green tree, you sprawled and served as a prostitute."

moment when each one of us also will face that final, definitive, "Yes" or "No" moment of decision. That moment is called death. Will we pass *our* test?

5. "GOD CREATES NEW ANGELS"

This is a final Christian misunderstanding about angels that needs correction. God does not give birth to new angels throughout time. There is a precise theological point at the base of this idea.

As purely spiritual beings, angels do not procreate through bodies as humans do, so God is their direct and only Creator. If we were to say that God creates new angels whenever He feels like it, we would be saying that God wasn't able to figure out the exact number of angels He needed when He thought about creating them in the first place.

Those who believe that God creates new angels have to wrestle with the total absence of any reference to the creation of angels in scripture or Tradition. We don't know when the angels were created.[29] The Church teaches only *that* they were created. There is no evidence that any more of them were created at any time.

The Christian Tradition holds the fair presumption that God created every single angel directly, all at once, according to His own design. And since angels cannot die, the first creation of angels was the only creation of angels.[30]

Ponder this for a minute: in a single brilliant burst of creative energy before human time began, God created every single angel that will ever exist. The billions (or trillions?) of angels all came into existence *at once*, fully formed, all of them utterly unique individuals and gloriously radiant in the magnificence of their beings.

The Big Bang that created our material world must have been like a pop gun in comparison to the Big Bright Burst of glory on that first day of the angels.

---

29 Most of the early Fathers of the Church thought that angels were created before the physical universe (Lang, *Angels*, 66-67). St. Augustine believed that the angels came to be at the moment when God said "Let there be light" (Gen 1:3). St. Thomas Aquinas taught that the angels and the world were created simultaneously. God has hidden this from us and we will only know the full truth in heaven.

30 Kreeft, *Angels (and Demons)*, 20.

3

NON-CHRISTIAN MYTHS ABOUT ANGELS

Many people these days describe themselves as "spiritual but not religious". Whenever I hear this misguided logic I'm tempted to respond, "Well, the devil is spiritual too – but definitely not religious. So your point is?"

This attitude has an effect on the way we see angels. Where people reject the hard truths of religion (Christianity in particular), angels are often little more than security blankets. People want angels to keep them warm without ever challenging them to repent of their sins. In this view, angels exist for comfort, not for salvation.

But angels are not comfortable beings. They are as far superior to us in strength and intelligence as we are to the smallest, weakest animals of our world. They are the antithesis of the warm, fuzzy, tantalizing creatures of greeting cards – and they certainly are not chubby babies with wings! They are raw truth and unsentimental charity.

Let's take a moment to bust a few myths about these messengers of grace so we don't fall prey to non-Christian illusions or cultural distortions.

1. NEW AGE MYTHS

Myth 1: "Angels are our friends"

I realize I'm getting myself into hot water by questioning the cherished belief that angels are our best buddies, so I decided to put this item first. How, exactly, can you have a friendship with an invisible, otherworldly being?

Angels don't comfortably fit into any activity or category we normally assign to friendship. We can talk to angels, ask their protection and help, etc., but these types of things are not specific to friendships only. When it comes to things we actually do with our friends – dining out, going on vacations, turning to them for emotional support, etc. – it's clear we don't do these things with angels.

It's easier to assign the qualities of friendship to creatures lower than us on the ladder of existence (I'll address this in Chapter 5). We call pets our friends because our companionship with them bears some similarities to human friendships (affection, fun, joy, loyalty, emotional support, etc.). These traits are tangible and identifiable as elements of friendship as we know it, but friendship with animals is also more of a metaphor than a reality when you think about it. Our human friends generally are not dependent upon us for their food, and we don't take them out for walks every day, do we?

Since angels are of a higher nature than humans, we're in uncharted relationship territory. Angels are immaterial and existentially superior. We innately sense their importance for our lives, but it's hard to put a term on what they mean to us, which is why we default to the familiar term friendship. We use friendship as a metaphor to try to bridge the existential distance separating our two natures. When we call angels our friends, we're really saying something different.

Let me use a human example to illustrate this.

Years ago I had the chance to attend a private Mass of Pope John Paul II in St. Peter's Basilica in Rome – an incredible experience! I was feet away from the great man the whole time. His deep blue eyes and rich voice, as well as his overwhelming presence there in the sanctuary, affected me deeply.

As I approached him to receive Communion, he said "Corpus Christi" as he offered me the sacred Host, and I can only describe that moment as a peak spiritual experience for me. For an instant, I was very closely connected with the visible head of my Church in the most meaningful form of prayer the Church offers.

Despite that one minute of connectedness with a saintly man, and despite our union in the faith, I would never presume to describe him as my friend. There was a very distinct distance separating us – cultural, intellectual, and even spiritual – which made me feel quite small and insignificant in his presence. Although the pope and I are *equal* in the eyes of God, the quality of his human culture and deep holiness far surpassed mine.

What does all this have to do with angels? Simple. It explains why angels were not created to be our friends. Friendship requires a certain equality in life interests, intelligence, culture, and circumstances. But no strict equality exists between a human being and an angel in any category: intelligence, power, virtue, holiness, mobility, vitality, authority, etc. We are of different natures. We live in different worlds. Angels are vastly superior to us in every way.

This is why angels are not our friends. The existential gap between us and them is too wide. The *Catechism* says that they "surpass in perfection all visible creatures, as the splendor of their glory bears witness."[31] We respect their power, their dignity, and their superior capacities, but we don't call them friends.

Peter Kreeft says that angels are always at our sides "as our bodyguards and soulguards. But not as servants or pets. If anything, we are like pets to them."[32] It would be better to think of angels as powerful watchmen, tutors, mentors, and guardians, and even warriors, a description that largely captures the human experiences of angels as revealed in scripture.

Here's the other side of that coin: demons are angels too. Imagine all that immense spiritual power turned *against* you.

Myth 2: "We can name our guardian angels"

The New Age is big on naming angels. (Many Christians fall prey to this illusion too.) Naming is taming in the occult world, but it's an illusion. God's angels will not be reduced to human terms or made subservient to our whims. They are not our kids or our pets.

---

31 *Catechism*, 330.
32 Kreeft, *Angels (and Demons)*, 59-60, 105.

Your guardian angel already has a name and would not make it known to you even if you asked.[33] This is further evidence that angels are not friends. How can you have a friend who won't tell you his name?

In their defense, there are a couple of good reasons angels don't want you to name them or know their names:

First, Christians name what we worship. God has revealed His Name to us for that reason. Celebrities and politicians may want us to worship them, but holy angels want no part of misguided worship so they don't let us know their names. Angels are glorious but not divine. This brings us to our second point.

Another reason the Church forbids naming angels is that it trivializes them and shrinks them to our level. It also leaves us open to the deception of demons (see Point 4 below). Here are two examples of how that can take place:

A lady I once knew said that she asked her guardian angel to reveal his name to her, and (allegedly) he told her his name was Frank. Do you find that as hard to believe as I do? Another lady I knew was given some bad advice in an RCIA program and felt she had permission to choose a nice name for her guardian angel. She focused on a Hebrew word she had heard in church. (It had to be okay if she heard it in church, right?) She didn't know the meaning of it but liked how it sounded, so she named her angel "Sheol" – which is the Hebrew word for *hell!* Madness of this kind distorts the true nature of angels.

While God is certainly free to allow an angel to reveal his name to a human being for a reason known only to God – encouragement, strength, salvation, etc. – it is not His normal policy. Angels for their part don't want us to get too fascinated with them and take our eyes off Christ.

Isn't it interesting that, even though the bible is full of angels, God has revealed only *three* of their names? The practice of naming implies authority or control over the one named, as in Adam naming the

---

33 See the stories of Jacob (Gen 32:29) and Samson's father, Manoah (Jdg 13:18), for an angel's refusal to give his name when asked.

animals in Genesis or parents naming their children. That's fine for those who are subject to our authority, but the idea that a human being might have authority over a superior angelic being is unbiblical, unwise, illogical, and extremely dangerous.

In 2001 the Congregation for Divine Worship and the Discipline of the Sacraments addressed this problem in terms that are diplomatic but firm: "The practice of assigning names to the Holy Angels should be discouraged, except in the cases of Gabriel, Raphael and Michael whose names are contained in Holy Scripture."[34]

The only occasion where the Church allows, in fact requires, asking the name of an angel is during an exorcism, but it's not about holy angels. The *Rite of Exorcism*[35] says that the priest must command the possessing demon to pronounce its name so that its presence will be exposed and brought more firmly under the authority of the Church.

2. MORMON MYTHS

"Humans can become angels and angels can become human" is a myth.

Another common misconception about angels – often reinforced by Hollywood[36] – is that they are some kind of re-cycled, spiritualized human beings. Humans share a spiritual nature with angels, of course, but angels never *become* human, nor do humans ever transform themselves into angels, even when they die. Angels are angels, humans are humans, and never shall their natures mix.

The Catholic position is based upon an understanding of the natural law. It holds that God has created each being in the universe with its own nature (unique identity), which makes that creature distinct from every other being in the universe and destined to remain that way

---

34 *Directory on Popular Piety and the Liturgy*, issued by the Congregation in 2001, n. 217.
35 Part I, n. 15 of the 1614 exorcism ritual; cf. Rev. Philip T. Weller, *The Roman Ritual, Vol. II, Christian Burial, Exorcisms, Reserved Blessings, Etc.*, (Milwaukee, WI: Bruce Publishing Co., 1964), 169-175.
36 The beloved 1946 movie, *It's a Wonderful Life* described Clarence Oddbody, George Bailey's guardian angel, as 293 years old and trying to "earn" his wings. As Peter Kreeft noted, the movie's director, Frank Capra, was a great moviemaker but not a great theologian.

forever. Because of that, natures are non-transferrable from one being to another.[37]

If you want to know how important the natural law is, just look at a religious system that is not based strictly on nature: Mormonism. Despite the many positive characteristics of their religion, Mormons have some rather serious angel/human issues.

According to the Mormon doctrine, there are certain entities that progress from one form of being to another:

> There are several types and kinds of beings, in various stages of progression, whom the LORD has used as angels in varying circumstances. One kind is a spirit child of the Eternal Father who has not yet been born on the earth but is intended for earthly mortality.[38]

Once you confuse the clear distinctions between human nature and angelic nature, you create a sort of hybrid spiritual/human entity that doesn't exist in reality. "Spirit children" are the equivalent of the centaurs and demi-gods of the ancient pagan religions.

Mormons also believe that angels can be transformed into flesh-and-blood humans sent to earth to do extraordinary tasks. In Mormon theology, for example, John the Baptist, most of the Apostles, as well as Moses and Elijah were actually angels, which means they were not really flesh-and-blood humans who performed their extraordinary acts of faith. This also is not a Christian belief.

Jesus taught that the saved will not be married in heaven but will "live like the angels" (Mt 22:30; Mk 12:25) after the resurrection of the dead. He was not saying that we would *become* angels after death but that we would "live like angels", which is an admirable goal to strive for even before we die. That humans become angels or that angels become human is simply not possible in God's universe.

---

37 This is also the reason why Catholics do not hold to the strict Theory of Evolution which believes one species can morph into another over time through natural processes.
38 Oscar W. McConkie, "Angels", http://eom.byu.edu/index.php/Angels, accessed 7/11/20.

3. THE JEHOVAH'S WITNESS MYTH

Perhaps the most interesting angelic heresy of all is the Jehovah's Witness belief[39] that Jesus pre-existed His earthly life as Michael the Archangel. After His Resurrection, they say, He returned to heaven and reverted to His prior existence as St. Michael. This is nothing more than spiritual gobbledygook.

The Witnesses do not believe in the Trinitarian God of Christianity. They identify God the Father as Jehovah of the Old Testament and make the Holy Spirit into some sort of impersonal source of energy in the universe. They understand that Jesus was a spiritual being, but they do not believe He is divine. Their teaching is not Christian, which is why their understanding of angels is also not Christian and not accurate.

So, when Jehovah's Witnesses come to your door peddling the Jesus-as-Michael myth, you should declare your firm belief in Christ's divinity and, with a polite smile, invite them in to pray the Rosary.

4. THE DANGEROUS OCCULT MYTH

For the moment, let's exclude the idea of personal prayer to our guardian angels, which is legitimate under certain conditions. (There is a "safe" way to do this, which I will address in the Conclusion.) The erroneous idea is that we can "make contact" with angels through various means other than authentic Christian prayer.

Believe me, when God wants you to meet an angel, the angel will be the one to initiate contact, not you.

There are several million reasons why we should not try to contact angels: *fallen angels*. Attempting to make contact with the spiritual world of angels potentially opens us to the influence of the seductive spirits we know as demons.

In the bible, plenty of people meet angels face to face, but nowhere do we find people of faith trying to make contact with angels by invoking them or demanding that they appear or asking them to do

---

39 Jehovah's Witnesses, *What Does the Bible Really Teach*, "St. Michael the Archangel", http://www.jw.org/en/publications/books/bible-teach/who-is-michael-the-archangel/, accessed 7/11/20.

something for them.[40] The nearest incident of this type is King Saul's infamous visit to the Witch of Endor, where he asked her to conjure up the spirit of the prophet Samuel (1 Sam 28:3-25). But that was a violation of every command of God as well as King Saul's own prohibition. The whole episode ended catastrophically for him, which is a lesson for us.

Both the bible and the Church issue severe warnings for us to stay away from all occult activity of any type. The warning is not a partial command. It is absolute. The Church's position is essentially a "No Contact Policy" regarding esoteric spiritual forces of which *we have little to no understanding*. The St. Michael Prayer asks God to free us from "the wickedness and snares of the devil" precisely because occult activities are the deceptions and traps demons use for the destruction of our souls.

This contact brings inevitable negative consequences for the participants, even if not immediately. I vividly recall being part of a prayer team some years ago where we prayed over a young man who was having spiritual problems. In the middle of our prayer, he began to chant in a low voice, and his body began to convulse up and down rhythmically. This went on for several minutes. It was hard to figure out what was happening.

Afterward, he told us that he had once attended a New Age ritual in the desert with a girlfriend, where the leaders invoked all kinds of Native American spirits upon the group. There was chanting and agitated dancing around a campfire that night, which explained what happened when we prayed for him. The man had opened himself to a spiritual invasion (sometimes called demonic oppression) because he attended an occult ritual. Christian prayer freed him from that demonic influence.

In the Old Testament, the people of Israel were always getting tangled up in the demonic religions of their pagan neighbors, which

---

40 Manoah in Judges 13:6 asks God to send "the man of God" back to him after an earlier visitation to his wife. Judith Lang says, "Manoah does not know he is asking to see an angel, but as such his prayer is unique in the Bible. Angels do not appear on demand, nor do people request to see them." Cf. *Angels of God*, 120.

caused an endless list of scathing rebukes from Moses and the prophets.[41] The prohibition is no less stern in the New Testament: "Do not be deceived," said St. Paul to the Corinthians, "neither fornicators nor *idolaters* nor adulterers ... will inherit the kingdom of God" (1 Cor 6:9-10).

The *Catechism* is a bit milder in its expressions but repeats those same prohibitions by listing concrete modern examples of occult influences to avoid:

> Consulting horoscopes, astrology, palm reading, interpretation of omens and lots, the phenomena of clairvoyance, and recourse to mediums all conceal a desire for power over time, history, and, in the last analysis, other human beings, as well as a wish to conciliate hidden powers. They contradict the honor, respect, and loving fear that we owe to God alone. (*Catechism*, 2116)

As I say: angels are incandescent fire. So are demons. Those who play with fire get burned.

---

41 Cf. Ex 20:2-4, 32:27f. See also Dt 5:6-7; Lev 19:4; 1 Sam 15:23; Is 44:9-20; Jer 11:12; Hos 11:2; Mi 5:13; Hab 2:18; Dan 5:23; and Mal 2:11-13, to name but a few.

4

TRUTHS ABOUT ANGELS IN THEMSELVES

What *are* angels, really? What makes angels tick? How do we understand their make-up, dynamism, and power?

Church teaching is quite mute on many of the fine points about angelic nature, so we have to rely on theological reasoning to answer these questions. To understand immaterial things, we must stretch the imagination, fill in the gaps, hypothesize, analogize, and theorize based upon what we already know about angels from Church teaching and faith.

This chapter presents a number of truths about the angels' existence that will help us better understand and appreciate these natures of fire.

1. ANGELIC UNIQUENESS

Many years ago, when I first got interested in angels, I was attending a Catholic college that offered a philosophy course on St. Thomas Aquinas. The great philosopher and theologian is known to Church history as the Angelic Doctor because of his extensive teaching about angels.

Right at the start of the section on angels, the professor said that angels were very lonely beings. One may imagine many things about angels, but loneliness is not usually what comes to mind.

The professor was trying to teach us a rather complex idea about angels: namely, that each angel is its own entirely distinct species. It means that every angel is as different from every other angel as we humans are different from other species of animals, such as cats, orangutans, and beetles. That's a mind-bender. (In Chapters 6 and 7 we'll talk about how angels can be grouped together despite being so different from one another.)

I haven't forgotten the discussion about angelic loneliness, but I prefer to call it angelic uniqueness. St. Thomas Aquinas based his theory of angel uniqueness on their *immateriality*. Since angels lack a physical body, they are different from everything we know about the world of nature and different from each other in striking ways.

In human or animal species, for example, the *material* element of our makeup allows a natural species to have many different members and many different categories within the same species. Closest to home, the species *homo sapiens,* for example, has not only seven and a half billion individual members, but also consists of many categories of human beings within the species (cultures, language groups, ethnicities, etc.).

Material differences such as skin color, body type, height, weight, etc. make possible millions of slightly different carbon copies of the species "human". Just think of the variety of faces in humanity, all of which incorporate the same elements of eyes, ears, mouth, nose, skin, etc. in different ways. All this diversity is possible because we are material beings.

But angels are immaterial. Without a material element as the principle of multiplication, they cannot have many members of the same species. This may seem bizarre to the human mind that thinks of species as groups, but it is not a problem for God – He made each angel its own species.

So, instead of angels relating to each other like members of a family or tribe (as in George, Grace, Gary and Gertrude) or like an animal cohort (such as Fido, Fifi, Furry, and Fluffy), angels relate to each other as species-distinct beings: kind of like amoeba, butterfly, cat, dromedary, emu, all the way to zebra (or however many angels exist).

Wild, right?

In essence, if a being is made of matter, there will be many more like him, each varying in a greater or lesser degree from all others. However, if a being is *not* made of matter, he has no relatives, in-laws, parents, brothers, or sisters. He is the exclusive member of his own species, with his own spiritual architecture and characteristics. Such are angels. This radical uniqueness of angel species leads us to the next discussion.

2. ANGELIC ARCHITECTURE

Each angel, as its own species, must be designed by God with a unique identity and beauty analogous to the differences in biological species. Even here, the comparison between animals and angels falls short. We can visualize the differences between an anteater and a zebra because we can see them or call up images of them whenever we want. We can't do that with invisible, immaterial beings except through the artistic imagination, which simply uses material categories to describe them. (We will discuss this subject in much greater detail in Chapters 10 and 11).

What are individual angelic species like? Even the biblical descriptions of angels are of little help because when angels appear to humans, they generally do so in forms that are recognizable to us. But such outward appearances are foreign to their nature. They are like costumes rather than real substances.

Even though we can't visualize the invisible, we can use analogies to understand what an invisible design might be like. Let's consider several wonders of human design, all of which should be easily recognizable to us:

- An engineering wonder: the Great Wall of China
- A technological wonder: the micro-processing chip
- A telecommunications wonder: the Internet

These are all human designs of immense scale.

But don't consider physical size alone in the evaluation of scale. Also consider the invisible element: power. Tiny structures like micro-processing chips are incredibly powerful when we consider their complexity and the amount of information processing potential contained in such a compressed space.

These extraordinary designs of man are radically complex, but they are also unified so that we can see each of them as one thing. For example, we don't speak of many internet systems but of "*the* Internet" or "the world wide web" (singular). We don't talk about the millions of stones used to build an extensive structure throughout northern China; we call it "the Great *Wall*". Even the microchip contains millions of transistors that are all combined to create a single "integrated circuit".

Now try to imagine *invisible* designs that contain within themselves an indestructible life force, creative purpose, commanding willpower, perfect unity, and surpassing intelligence. Like with the micro-processor: don't think size, think power.

Try to imagine something that has an even greater power and capacity than the Internet but has no need for computer hardware, servers, and electrical cords or radio waves to deliver that power. Now we're getting close to understanding spiritual power.

Furthermore, angel designs make the angels perfectly suited for their particular functions. The microchip, for example, works perfectly when embedded in the central processing unit of a computer but would be a tiny speck of metallic junk anywhere else. The Great Wall of China running along ridges at the bottom of the ocean would be worthless to anyone.

In the same way, each angel has a design suited *exactly* to the mission for which God created him. The Seraphim, for example, are always pictured *as fire* because they are closest to God and burn with intense charity.[42] The Principalities are named for "princes" because their particular mission is to rule over entire nations.

Fill these beings with light and glory, intelligence and holiness, and you get a glimpse of the powerful spiritual creatures we know as angels.

---

42 Incidentally, the Hebrew root for this name is "saraph", which means "to burn". More on angel classifications in Chapters 6 and 7.

Of course it's hard to imagine what lies beyond the reach of our five senses. Human minds appreciate the achievements of man, but we cannot truly fathom the beauty and scope of spiritual architecture, whose designs run into the billions and perhaps trillions of different angelic models.

That is one of the many reasons I long for heaven. I can't wait to see the mystical architecture and light show of all those angels.

3. ANGELIC MINDS

How exactly does the mind of an angel work?

To start with, the angelic mind does not work like the human mind. For the sake of argument, let's pretend that all human beings think rationally and logically (a tall order, I know).

Angel minds don't reason. They intuit. This means that angels understand things *immediately* when they turn their minds to them, whereas human beings have to arrive at an understanding of things through a rational process. You may recall we said in Chapter 1 that angels have a "full hard drive" of natural knowledge as part of their makeup. All knowledge of the world is already in them. All they have to do is turn their minds to (pay attention to, focus on) any part of God's creation to access a full understanding of it. Another human analogy may help here:

People of a certain age will remember the old Polaroid cameras. Taking a picture with a Polaroid was fun, but getting the fully developed picture meant going through a certain process. Once you snapped the shot, the undeveloped photo paper would slide out the front of the camera, and you would wait eagerly as the little square of photo-sensitive paper developed into an actual photo of a real life scene. The picture literally "came to life" in about a minute-and-a-half.

This is analogous to the way the human mind works. When the mind fixes on something (like a camera snap), it normally requires a process of questioning, reasoning, learning, engaging with the object (like the photo development) to come to a clearer understanding of it (the completely developed picture). We call that function of the mind reasoning or understanding, and it's always a process.

Angels need no such process to know things. When their minds focus on something (snap), they understand the whole of it immediately (snap), like a digital camera. The picture and the click of the camera are one.

Why the difference between the two types of minds? It has to do with our spirit-and-body makeup. Human minds are bound to the flesh. Angelic minds are not. Flesh-minds, if you will, operate through the human senses, the organ of the brain, and within the flow of chronological time. They need sense data to get a picture of something, and they arrive at understanding slowly, like the development of a Polaroid photo.

Angel-minds, on the other hand, operate within the realm of spirit. They are not bound to the human brain and do not gain data through the senses (because they do not have senses). They exist outside of time and look upon things as a whole rather than learning about them through a collection of partial understandings that develop incrementally into a full picture.

This means that angels can know entire languages instantly (with all the slang expressions, accents, and dialects that go with them). Amazing! It means that any angel who turns his mind to engineering could design and build a better car, computer, bridge, skyscraper, city, or space station than any human engineer ever could.

But angels aren't interested in human structures, they're interested in saving human souls. All their mental and spiritual powers are dedicated to this great mission.

We should be grateful that the holy angels are our allies because the demons have those types of powerful minds too. Those wicked minds have one singular focus: our destruction.

4. ANGELIC GENDER

As spiritual beings, there are no male or female angels as such because angels do not have physical bodies to manifest the differences of sex. Still, I fully agree with the opinion of C.S. Lewis that there is probably *gender* in angels, or at least characteristics we may interpret as masculinity and femininity.[43] The Church has no formal teaching on angelic gender but allows speculation on this fascinating subject.

We must start with one huge caveat, though. There are no angels in scripture that resemble females, either in form or in dress. The Greek word for angel, *angelos*, has no feminine cognate, and no angel is ever referred to by the pronouns "she" or "her" throughout scripture. Believe me, I've scoured the bible from cover to cover. Female angels just can't be found.

The evidence of saints who regularly saw or conversed with angels confirms that angels take on masculine form, manner, or dress when they appear. The Angel of Peace seen by the seers at Fatima was male. Padre Pio's guardian angel was a little boy. Gemma Galgani's angel was a rather severe masculine figure. St. Joan of Arc spoke to St. Michael the Archangel, whereas her other visions were of female saints. St. Martin of Tours and St. Faustina each had visions of their (male) guardian angels. Most fascinating of all, St. Frances of Rome's vision of hell included no female demons, just the bad boys of the spiritual world.

Peter Kreeft notes that all angels that appear in the Old Testament, the New Testament, and even the Koran, are masculine because they are warriors and messengers,[44] which, in the ancient world, were roles exclusively reserved to men. Angels also appear as masculine and powerful because they represent God who reveals Himself primarily in masculine terms in scripture.

Does this mean there are no female/feminine angels? Not at all. It just means that we have no revelation about them from scripture or Church Tradition.

If we were able to discern more closely the personalities of angels, we might notice in them certain features of masculinity and femininity

---

43 Kreeft, *Angels (and Demons)*, 76-78. These differentiating qualities of personality seem to be reflected across the spectrum of creatures throughout the natural world, quite contrary to modern gender theory.

44 The origin of the word "angel" is circuitous: the Sanskrit word "angeres" was adopted into the Persian language as "angaros" meaning "courier". From there the Greeks appropriated the word and made it into "angellos" – messenger – and the Romans then took it whole into the Latin lexicon as "angelus", whence we get our word "angel". The Hebrew Bible's name for angel is "mal'akh" (messenger), which has no direct English equivalent. Cf. Godwin, *Endangered Species*, 66.

that we associate with human gender differences. We would discern these characteristics in the way the angels act, the way they speak, and in the way they *are*. We won't get a chance to make that evaluation this side of heaven.

Here's a final thought on gender. Males in the animal kingdom are typically more beautiful and colorful than females, probably because the females must blend into their natural environments more effectively for the protection of the young. That's the way of the animal world. In the realm of the hybrid spiritual beings we call humans, however, the trend is reversed; females are more beautiful than males.

It's likely, then, that in the realm of the *highest* spiritual beings, the angels, the greatest beauty will take the form of angelic femininity. Perhaps God saved His greatest angelic masterpieces for last, as He did in the creation story (Gen 2:18-25), where the pinnacle of human creation was Eve. It's just speculation, of course, but if the masculine angels of scripture are so glorious, what must feminine angels be like?

5. ANGELIC MUSIC

Pious imagination throughout history has frequently associated angels with music (angel choirs, angels playing instruments, etc.), yet there is little direct biblical evidence for it. We have a few suggestions of angelic music in the Old and New Testaments.[45] Most direct references to the music of angels are found in the Book of Revelation.

John said that he "heard the voices of many angels who surrounded the throne" (Rev. 5:11) as the whole assembly of angels and elect humans sang a hymn of adoration to the Lamb of God. The term "singing", however, is incorrect. New Testament Greek actually uses the word "saying" or "speaking" (*legontes*) to describe this angelic activity (Rev 5:9.11.12), as if their mode of music is more like *chanting* or *harmonizing* than singing. Virtually every version of the bible translates these verses as, "they cried out in a loud voice, *saying*...."

---

45 These are intimations only, not solid evidence. Cf. Job 38:7 concerning the singing of the stars at their creation, and the Seraphim crying out "glory" to one another in the Temple of Heaven (Is 6:3). Virtually all references to music-making in the Old and New Testaments have to do with humans.

The use of the Greek verb for "singing" (*adousin*) in Rev 5:9 only refers to the human saints who "sang a new song" in adoration of the Lamb.[46] The Greek word for "singing" is never applied to angels in these passages. And sorry, despite its popularity in art and culture, the word "singing" isn't used for the angel choirs that appeared on the night of Our LORD's birth (Lk 2:13-14). *Singing* seems to be an exclusively human activity requiring vocal chords

Perhaps the association of angels with music comes from the idea of music as the universal language.[47] Many creative geniuses throughout history have made music to uplift the human spirit, sometimes reaching sublime heights of expression. George Frideric Handel said of the audience of his greatest masterpiece, *The Messiah*: "I should be sorry if I only entertained them; I wished to make them better." If angels did not have a hand in the greatest masterpieces of music, especially religious music, it would be hard to conceive of such genius as mere human talent alone.

Great religious music throughout the centuries must certainly be angelically-inspired, particularly liturgical music. We can easily believe in a sort of mystical coordination between humans and angels in their greatest service to God, which is adoration. We have enduring traditions of religious music – Gregorian chant, the great Akathistos hymns of Eastern Christianity, the sublime polyphonic *a capella* music of the Ukrainian and Russian churches, etc. – as confirmation of this idea.

Ancient and medieval philosophers taught that "the order of the heavens, kept by the angelic spheres, is so harmonious that it produces a beautiful music, each sphere with its own note."[48] This idea of angelic creativity through music endures to the modern day in the religious mind. J.R.R. Tolkien wrote in his masterful work, *The Silmarillion*,

---

46 Singing, in a human sense, requires physical vocal chords, which angels do not have; hence, the more accurate analogy for angelic musical performance is *chanting* or *harmonizing*. The bible, in all cases, uses the Greek verb "speaking" or "saying" (*legontes*) rather than "singing" to describe this angelic activity.

47 Graham, *Angels*, 49.

48 Lang, *Angels*, 175.

that the angels brought the world into being through their harmonious praise of God.[49]

If angels are constantly associated with music, why do we not hear angel music? Once again, the problem remains with us. We are simply not spiritual or pure enough. A medieval English mystic, Walter Hilton, made this observation:

> No soul may truly feel the angels' song nor heavenly sound unless it is in perfect charity. And not all that are in perfect charity feel it, but only that soul that is purified in the fire of love of God, that all earthly savour is burned out of it and all obstacles between the soul and the cleanness of angels are broken down and put away from it. Then may he sing a new song, and may he hear a blissful heavenly sound and angels' song without deceit or feigning.[50]

Here we come upon the ongoing problem when sinful human beings try to relate to angels: we are just not spiritual (holy) enough to perceive them clearly.

---

49 "In this Music the World was begun; for Iluvatar made visible the song of the Ainur [angels], and they beheld it as a light in the darkness." *GoodReads.com*, "The Silmarillion Quotes", accessed on 7/20/20.

50 Lang, *Angels*, 175, citing Walter Hilton, *Of Angels' Song*, from the Middle English.

5

TRUTHS ABOUT ANGELS IN RELATION TO US

The wildly famous series known as *Chicken Soup for the Soul* has more than two hundred and fifty titles, each of which features 101 distinct stories on an impressive range of subjects. What's more, the series includes at least *five* books about people who have had direct experiences of angels!

Many people have met their guardian angels face to face. Angels rescue them, instruct them, warn them, or affect their lives in some significant way. Some of these stories are written from the context of faith, but not all of them. It's amazing how the secular world confirms the teaching of the Church time and again.

The mission of guardian angels is to accompany us on the journey of life and help us get to heaven, so we must examine what the Church has to say about the interaction of angels with the world of human beings.

1. ANGEL PLACEMENT

Let's start with the most fundamental question: why do angels exist *at all*?

If you're an atheist or a pure materialist you don't think they do. Fine. But some of the greatest minds in history – thinkers like Plato,

Aristotle, Aquinas, Maimonides, Averroës, and Niels Bohr – beg to differ with you. There is only one person on that list who is a canonized saint, so the Catholic objection isn't going to cut it. Two were pagans, two others were Jewish and Islamic philosophers, and the last one was a Nobel-Prize-winning, Danish physicist. So we've got the ancient, medieval, and modern ages covered.

The basic rationale of the angels' existence is this: they complete God's grand masterwork of creation, part of which is immaterial. That is, if angels didn't exist, there would be a huge hole in the universe. Not a hole in space, like a black hole, but a hole in the very makeup of the universe itself.

Here's what this means. The ancient philosophers discerned a sort of mystical ladder of existence stretching from the lowest creatures to the highest beings in the universe. (We're back to the existential question again.) So, there is an ascending and descending scale of beings in the universe, with some having more *existence* than others. Ascending and descending is probably why they referred to it as a ladder of existence.[51]

In Chapter 2 we discussed time and space in relation to the angels, but the ancients also thought a lot about the dignity, vitality, and power of everything that exists, from low to high. The following chart should make this clear. (You can read further on this very interesting subject if you wish.)[52]

---

[51] It is also referred to as the "Great Chain of Being".
[52] See the Bibliography for the books by Mortimer Adler and Peter Kreeft especially, or simply do an Internet search for the "Great Chain of Being".

THE LADDER OF EXISTENCE

Being / Entity	Existential Characteristics	Dignity-Vitality-Power
God	Omniscient-Omnipresent-Omnipotent	Source of all that exists
Angels	Purely Spiritual	Intellectual[53]
Humans	Material / Spiritual	Rational / Self-Aware
Animals	Material with Life and Consciousness	Instinctual / Mobile
Plants	Material with Life	Living
Raw Matter	Purely Material	None

Now let's pretend for a moment that the angels did not exist. The ladder of existence would be missing a rung:

"EXISTENTIAL" CHARACTERISTICS	
Omniscient-Omnipresent-Omnipotent[54]	
↑	The gap in the universe where the "purely spiritual" created existence should be.
Material / Spiritual	
Material with Life and Consciousness	
Material with Life	
Purely Material	

---

53 St. Thomas Aquinas described angels as "intellectual substances", which is a philosophical way of saying that they are minds without bodies.

54 As I mentioned in Chapter 2, it's not correct to put God into a list of other beings since He is the Source of all existence. I only do so here for the purpose of illustrating the "gap".

We humans may think we're special, but we're not *that* close to God. Is it possible that God could have created a world without purely spiritual beings? Yes, it's possible. Is it likely? No.

An invisible world of spiritual beings exists between the material world and God. We know this by faith, but it is also logical. The progression of existence from a purely time-bound, lifeless, material world at one end to the eternal Creator of all things at the other would have to include purely spiritual beings somewhere in that progression. Human beings are *partly* spiritual, but we do not share the full capacities of spirit. Angels do, yet they are not God.

As I said, if the angels did not exist, there would be a huge hole in the universe. God placed them on that ladder just where He wanted them.

2. ANGELIC APPEARANCE

If angels are such glorious creatures in themselves, why is it that they always seem to show up in human form? Why would a superior being like an angel want to put on the guise of a lower creature?

The reality is that sinful human beings normally would be overwhelmed by a direct experience of an angel's nature. So, like turning down the brightness on the screen of your smart phone, angels put on a costume and tone down the intensity of their glory when appearing to human beings. They usually do that by dressing up as one of us. Pretty clever.

The scriptural evidence for this is clear in any case. The angels who appeared to Abraham, Lot, Hagar, Jacob, Gideon, Joshua, Balaam, Tobit, Daniel, Mary, Zechariah, Peter, Paul, and the women at Jesus' Tomb, all appeared in human form. In many of these instances, the recipients of the vision bowed down or fell down in terror at the mere *human* appearance of the angel.[55]

My favorite account of human reactions to an angel sighting is in

---

[55] Appearing in human form seems to be characteristic only of angels and archangels, who are closest to man and dedicated to serving our spiritual welfare. Other angels in scripture appear as fire (the pillar of fire that protected the Israelites); chariots and horses (Elijah); wheels and thunder (Ezekiel); mighty four-headed creatures (Revelation) and other mysterious beings (Isaiah's Seraphim, among others).

the Book of Daniel. One day when Daniel was praying with some friends by a river in Babylon, he looked up and saw the figure of a "man". Even though his friends didn't see the vision, he said that "great fear seized those who were with me; they fled and hid themselves". Daniel himself "lost all strength" and "turned the color of death and was powerless". Then when the angel spoke, Daniel "fell face forward unconscious" (Dan 10:5-9). This is the effect of an angel's *muted* glory.

In Chapter 3, I mentioned that angels never transform themselves into humans. When angels appear to men, they *adopt* a human form without changing their essential nature. Taking on the appearance, speech, and mannerisms of humans is like an elaborate costume change for angels, usually for some distinct and time-limited purpose.[56] They "put on" a human appearance like an article of clothing over their angelic form.

Humans put on uniforms to go to work or dress up for an important event, but clothes are not substantial to human bodies; they only cover and augment the person's bodily features. Uniforms may also symbolize a person's vocation or profession (such as police, clergy, nurse, etc.) as an outward sign of their function.

Clothing, in a metaphorical sense, works the same way with angels. While an angel's adopted body looks, acts, sounds, and perhaps feels[57] like an authentic human body, it is not an *organic* body with all the functions of a material, human organism. It is only an elaborate, mystical costume.

We have biblical testimony about this phenomenon, too. In the Book of Tobit, when the Archangel Raphael reveals his true nature to Tobias and Tobit, he informs them: "Even though you saw me eat and drink, I did not eat or drink anything; what you were seeing was a vision" (Tob 12:19). In contrast, Jesus uses eating and drinking after His Resurrection to prove that He is not a vision, an angel, or a ghost.

---

56 There are no long-term or extended appearances of angels in the bible. Even the longest single angelic appearance in Scripture – that of the Archangel Raphael in the Book of Tobit – was limited and may have been intermittent (coming and going) rather than continuous.

57 St. Joan of Arc said she had touched the garments of the two female saints that appeared to her, but she never claimed to have touched her other visitor from heaven, St. Michael the Archangel. In theory, if an angel can create the visual illusion of a body, he could also create the tactile illusion of the solid feel of a human body, but as far as I know, there is no testimony to this in Church history.

As to how the angels create their amazing costumes, it's anyone's guess. (Another thing I'm going to ask St. Thomas when I meet him.)

3. ANGELIC COMMUNICATION

"If I speak in human and angelic tongues but do not have love, I am a resounding gong or a clashing cymbal," writes St. Paul in 1 Corinthians 13:1. St. Paul believed in angelic speech because the Old Testament scriptures and other Jewish literature written prior to the New Testament contained stories about angelic language, dialects, singing, etc.[58]

Yet, common sense tells us that angels have the power of language because all intelligent beings, even animals, are able to make their wishes known in some way. It's the form of communication that varies from one nature and species to another.

Angels do not speak with vocal chords or even with *words*, which are a means of human communication. They prefer to take the high road and communicate by virtue of their powerful intellects, through *ideas*. Angel communication is idea-to-mind, not word-to-mind as such. Our term for this is mental telepathy.

The way this happens is that an angel *wills a thought* to another angel, which is received or captured by the mind of the other angel. Since angelic minds are intuitive, an angel can "see" or envision every idea that is willed to him and grasp it whole as soon as he receives it. It's like what happens when a "light goes on" in our minds. When we finally understand something, we generally respond, "Oh, yes; I *see* what you mean now." This intuitive understanding, idea-to-mind or mind-to-mind, is angelic communication.

In contrast, human flesh-minds go through a laborious word-to-mind process when we communicate. Even if you leave out the possibility of confusion, normal human verbal communication is a four-step process:[59]

---

58 Irene Nowell, OSB, *101 Questions & Answers on Angels and Devils* (Mahwah, NJ: Paulist Press, 2012), 20-21.

59 Based on the concept of the "two translations" in E.F. Schumacher, *A Guide for the Perplexed* (NY: Harper & Row Publishers, Inc., 1977), 81 ff.

- The idea in the mind of one person takes the form of a word;
- The mouth speaks the word;
- The ear of the other person captures the sound waves of the spoken word; and
- The receiver's mind translates that idea into an understanding of the other person's *meaning*.

At any stage of this process, our communication can be skewed or distorted (by fatigue, misunderstandings, blockages, emotions, etc.) and the meaning lost, which is why human beings are generally pretty bad communicators. It's not a simple process!

Communicating by way of ideas, on the other hand, is much simpler. It cuts out all the intermediary elements (such as human organs of speech and hearing) so no word or human mechanism distorts the communication. One angel transmits the idea in his mind, and the other angel understands instantaneously and perfectly the *meaning* communicated to him from the other mind.

Even a dull human mind can understand an angel idea when the angel chooses to communicate with him. The angel may communicate his idea without human words (by mental telepathy), or he may choose to communicate by means of human words (that is, in something that is recognized by the ear or mind as an audible "voice"), depending on the circumstances of his particular mission.[60]

One final item: angels do not play games with language. They never sit around and chit-chat with humans. With the exception of Gabriel's long speech in Chapter 10 of Daniel (which is a prophecy), angels speak to humans in the form of short commands or pronouncements, not casual communications, suggestions, commentaries, or musings.[61]

---

60 See Augustin Poulain, SJ, Leonora L. Yorke Smith, tr., *Revelations and Visions: Discerning the True and the Certain from the False or the Doubtful* (NY: Alba House, 1998), 6-9, concerning the pitfalls of discerning angel communications and interior locutions.

61 Take a look at how angels speak to Gideon (Jdg 6:12-14); Samson's mother (Jdg 13:2-3); Joshua (Josh 5:13-6:60); Peter (Acts 5:19-20; 10:9-23.30-33); and John (Rev 17:1; 19:9-11), and you will see this point amply illustrated.

Angels never mince or waste words. They command. They don't fool around when it comes to doing God's will. Nor should we.

4. ANGELIC WINGS

Many New Age "angel seers" or self-proclaimed mystics believe they can feel the brush of angel wings as they fly by. This is illusory thinking. It's a kind of trivial behavior that the angels do not indulge in, and there is no scriptural evidence of this ever happening.

With regard to angel wings, the bible depicts only the two highest orders of angels, those closest to God, as winged beings. Any human who got near to these angels or their wings would probably melt.

Case in point: the prophet Isaiah is the only human being in the bible who had direct contact with the Seraphim, and he nearly died from the encounter (Is 6:5). Ezekiel had a similar reaction when he saw the Cherubim, each of which had four faces and four wings with all kinds of other mystical trimmings: "Such was the appearance of the likeness of the glory of the LORD. And when I saw it, I fell on my face…" (Ez 1:28), he said.

Except for these two classes of higher angels, there are no other angels in scripture that are described as having wings. Two passages (Dan 9:21 and Rev 14:6) describe angels as "flying" – metaphorical language for angelic movement – but neither of these passages indicate that the angels do so by means of wings.[62]

Flying and wings go together in the material world (except for Superman, of course!), but there is no necessary connection between flight and wings with spiritual beings. According to the biblical account, the Cherubim use their wings for covering, for connecting one angel to another, and for making noise (Ez 1:23-24). These wings seem to have no purpose of flight at all.

Wings are not included in the standard issue uniforms of the lower angels. Warrior angels with gigantic eagle wings, teenage girl angels with delicate swan wings, chubby baby angels with tiny bird wings, maternal winged presences with halos watching over children as they

---

[62] Lang, *Angels of* God, 210, 223.

cross rickety bridges, etc. – these are all Hallmark versions of angels, not the angels of scripture.

How do we explain the wings of the highest angels, then?

Wings symbolize the *magnificence* of the most powerful angels and their missions. Like nature's most majestic birds, these angels soar above all the others of their kind. Magnificent birds of prey are some of the most impressive creatures in the world of nature, so we can imagine that the mightiest creatures of a purely *spiritual* nature, the Cherubim and Seraphim, would be simply overwhelming in glory if we could behold them with our own eyes. Wings symbolize their innate splendor.

Human language has difficulty expressing mystical experiences, so we use symbols and metaphors to describe the indescribable. Religious imagination puts wings on angels to symbolize their swiftness in the service of God, their immediacy of action, their spiritual nature, and their lack of ties to the material world. Secular society puts wings on angels because they're cool and can be dressed up to fit the touchy-feely purposes of pop culture. This same culture also likes to put bat wings on demons.

On that matter, demons are nowhere depicted in the bible as having wings or flying. Notwithstanding popular depictions in great epic stories (like Tolkein's LORD *of the Rings)*, the biblical *dragons* – symbols of the devil – don't have wings either.[63] The Book of Job contains an extensive description of a dragon but lacks even the slightest reference to wings (Job 41:7-26). And that terrible red dragon in Chapter 12 of Revelation – he's wingless.

Despite this fact, Christian artists often represent the devil and other demons as having membranous bat wings, which is just another attempt to symbolize the corrupt nature of demons as fallen angels. All descriptions of demonic wings of any type are non-biblical.

5. ANGELS AFTER DEATH

It's legitimate to ask what happens to our guardian angels after we die. Are they recycled? Given a new job? Transferred to another post?

---

[63] The Hebrew and Greek words for "dragon" (*tannyin* and *drakon*) are found twenty-eight times in the Old Testament and eleven times in the New Testament, exclusively in the Book of Revelation. Not one of them has wings.

On permanent vacation? And what happens if a person goes to hell? Does his guardian angel get *fired*?

There are no direct answers to these questions in Christian doctrine, but there is a sort of theological logic that serves as a guide to understanding this mystery.

First, the gospels are clear that the angels have a role in bringing deceased souls to heaven. The story about the beggar Lazarus, who died at the gate of the rich man, ends with the consoling thought that the "angels carried him to the bosom of Abraham" (Lk 16:22). Some of the most dramatic Christian artwork shows angels in their role of ushering souls from this earthly life to heaven.

That part of the angels' ministry is at least clear. Your guardian angel has the task of hauling you before the judgment seat of God when you die. Will he be there to support you in your personal trial by fire? The Church provides no answer to this question, but it's likely that he will step out of the room and let God do all the talking.

Famed Catholic author Monsignor Charles Pope notes that Tradition lays out a number of possibilities for a guardian angel after his charge's death and judgment.[64] "If a soul enters communion with God," he says, "it joins its angel in praising the one and triune God for all eternity." Since one of the primary responsibilities of all angels is worship, that's a likely occupation of an angel that has finished his earthly task.

What if a soul must spend time in Purgatory? Will his angel go there with him? That also is both possible and likely. Our guardian angels have a role in making us fit to enter the Kingdom of God, so their job is not complete until the soul enters its eternal destiny. They probably either accompany us through the purifying fires of Purgatory or they intercede for us before the throne of God while we are being purified.

Somewhat more problematic for the angel is the possibility of the soul's eternal damnation: "If the soul goes to Hell," says Msgr. Pope, "its angel can only praise God's divine justice and holiness." In other words, the angel of a lost soul returns to his duty of worship, while focusing primarily on the righteousness of God's judgments.

---

[64] Msgr. Charles Pope, "The Angels and Our Death", *Catholic Standard*, 2/10/2019.

Does the angel lament the loss of that soul? Yes and no. Since angels don't have human emotions,[65] their reaction to the loss of souls would not be one of human grief. An angel may experience a truthful awareness akin to regret at the loss of something so precious, but he would not lament the loss as a personal failure.

Humans often blame themselves after a tragedy if they could have done something to prevent such a loss. But angels never fail in their duties, so a guardian angel does not reproach himself if his charge voluntarily chooses to separate himself from God for all eternity. That is not the angel's fault in any way.

Does a guardian angel get another soul to guard or get assigned other duties (other than worship) when his work is done? Msgr. Pope says that since there is such a vast number of angels, a new assignment "seems unlikely."

---

65 Recall that angels are purely spiritual beings. They have mind and will as we do, but not emotions, which are that part of the human soul that is bound to the flesh.

6
ANGELIC ORGANIZATIONS

My college professor who told us that angels are lonely beings forgot to mention one very important fact about angelic life. Angels in the bible almost always appear and act *in concert with other angels*.

This concept might seem strange to anyone who sees guardian angels as individual, personal protectors, but there is plenty of biblical evidence for angelic groupings, which the Book of Hebrews describes charmingly as "myriads of angels in festal gathering" (Heb 12:22). Consider just a few of them in the following chart:

SCRIPTURE	INCIDENT	NUMBER
Old Testament		
Genesis 18	Angels visit Abraham and Sarah to announce a future child	Three
Genesis 19	Angels visit and destroy Sodom and Gomorrah	Two
Genesis 28	Jacob saw angels ascending and descending a ladder	Multiple
2 Kings 2	A band of angels took Elijah up to heaven in a fiery chariot	Multiple

NATURES OF FIRE

SCRIPTURE	INCIDENT	NUMBER
2 Kings 6	Elisha showed Gehazi angels arrayed as horses and chariots on the mountainside	Multiple
Job 38:7	The angels rejoiced when God created the heavens	Multiple
Isaiah 6	Isaiah's vision of Seraphim in the Temple	Multiple
Ezekiel 1	Ezekiel's vision of Cherubim by the River Chebar	Multiple
Daniel 10	Archangels Michael and Gabriel appear together	Two
New Testament		
Matthew 13	Angels will separate the weeds from the wheat at the end of time	Multiple
Matthew 25	Jesus refers to "the devil and his angels"	Multiple
Mark 1	Angels wait on Jesus in the desert after His temptation	Multiple
Luke 2	Choirs of angels appear to the shepherds to announce the birth of Jesus	Multiple
Luke 5	The angels in Heaven rejoice when a sinner converts	Multiple
John 1	The disciples will see angels ascending and descending upon the Son of Man	Multiple
John 20	Two angels appear to Mary Magdalene at Jesus' tomb	Two
Ephesians 1	Dominions, Virtues, Powers, Principalities	Choirs
Colossians 1	Thrones, Dominions, Powers, Principalities	Choirs
Jude 6	Refers to the rebel angels who were cast out of heaven	Multiple

I didn't include the angels of the Book of Revelation in this chart because that book really needs a chart of its own. It is filled with duos, trios, quartets, teams, brigades, coalitions, and armies of angels working together for God and His Kingdom.

This is not to say that angels always operate in groups. Many angels in the bible are sole practitioners with focused missions and single appearances. We can name just a few of the more familiar ones: the angel who wrestled with Jacob (Gen 32); the angel who appeared to Elijah in the desert (1 Kgs 17); the angel who rescued the apostles from prison (Acts 5), among others.

The list of the many angel groups, however, does show that angelic ministries to humans can sometimes be more than the work of lone guardian angels. In fact, more often than not, their work is communal, and in order to do their ministries effectively, they have to be organized. Let's consider a few of these groupings.

1. ARMIES

The most common collective term for angels in the bible is "hosts". This can be translated literally from the Hebrew as "armies".[66] So all those pictures of angels in military garb were right after all!

The military analogy best describes angelic roles in the governance of the universe and in protecting the faithful. These groups are like the armed forces of a nation, each with its own realm of authority and action: Army, Navy, Marines, Air Force, National Guard, Coast Guard, Merchant Marine (and now the Space Force!). Other "hosts" of local police and law enforcement agencies protect their communities as well.

The Book of Revelation depicts a complete assembly of angels around the LORD's throne in heaven adoring the Lamb (Rev 5:11). There, the angelic hosts are in full force. The most striking reference comes at the end of the book where "the armies of Heaven" ride in the train of their commander, "the King of Kings and LORD of LORDS", as He slays the unrepentant pagan nations with the sword of His mouth

---

66 The term "Lord of Hosts" or "Lord of Armies" appears 250 times in the Bible. Jeremiah, *Who They Are*, 65. See especially the use of "hosts" in 1 Chr 18:18 and Ps 148:2. This word retains its meaning even in modern Hebrew. The Israeli Defense Forces use it (in the singular: Tsvah) in their official title.

(Rev. 19:11-16). Scenes like that make us appreciate what it means to "be on the side of the angels."

How many angels are there, exactly?

The bible never specifies the exact number of angels. Like angelic "time" (see Chapter 2), this is another mystery that we can barely wrap our minds around. Whenever biblical authors attempt to describe the number of angels, they always seem to stumble on their words. They use Semitic and Greek metaphors like "myriads upon myriads" (Dan 7:10), or "thousands upon thousands and ten thousand times ten thousand" (Rev 5:11)[67] to describe the number of God's soldiers.

If we calculate that last expression – 10,000 x 10,000 – we come up with one hundred million, which seems like a lot of angels, but it can't be the actual number. The Church teaches that each human being on earth has a guardian angel, so the minimum number of angels required *for that task alone today* would be 7.5 billion, not to mention the angels of all those who have gone before us! Like quasi-time measurements for angelic time, the biblical authors must use symbolic numbers to represent the immensity of angel hosts.

St. Michael's war with Satan, described in Revelation 12, illustrates a kind of militaristic role of angels in the divine government. Michael and his angels decisively put down the rebellion of the apostate angels by casting their leader, Satan, down to earth with all his minions. The angelic army restored order in heaven by the power of God and the leadership of the great Archangel, Michael. It was the one and only exorcism of heaven.

2. THE NINE CHOIRS

Apart from armies, no other theory of angelic organization has had such remarkable acceptance in the history of Christianity as the theory of the nine choirs. Our belief in angels is an article of faith, but our view of how they're organized is not.[68] It's just a good theory.

It probably owes its endurance to the fact that the names of the nine choirs are scriptural, particularly in St. Paul's writings but also in numerous

---

67 A literal rendering by the NAB (1970), as well as the NIV and the various King James Versions.
68 Cf. H. Pope, "Angels." *The Catholic Encyclopedia*. New York: Robert Appleton Company, 1907; http://www.newadvent.org/cathen/01476d.htm, accessed 7/12/20.

other places of the Old and New Testaments. Although the sacred writers use many different names to describe angels in the bible – "messengers", "mediators", "sons of God", "watchers", "servants", "hosts", "holy ones", etc.,[69] – theologians have consolidated this diversity of names into nine categories to create a kind of organizing template for angelic groups.

The chart below lists the nine choirs and the places where each is referenced in scripture. (See Appendix 2 for a fuller description of each of the choirs' identities and functions).[70] The nine choirs are ranked here from the highest (most powerful and intelligent) to the lowest (least powerful and intelligent) angels in the traditional list:

THE NINE CHOIRS OF ANGELS	
Choir	Scripture Reference
1. Seraphim (singular, "Seraph")	Is 6:1-7
2. Cherubim (singular, "Cherub")	Gen 3:24; Sir 49:8; Pss 17:11, 80:2, 99:1; Is 37:16; Ez 1:10; Dan 3:55; Rev 4-7, 14-15, 19
3. Thrones	Dan 7:9; Col 1:16
4. Dominions (or "Dominations")	Eph 1:21; Col 1:16
5. Virtues	Rom 8:38; 1 Cor 15:24; Eph 1:21; 1 Pt 3:22
6. Powers	1 Cor 15:24; Eph 1:21; Eph 3:10; Eph 6:11; Col 1:16; Col 2:10; Col 2:15; 1 Pt 3:22
7. Principalities	Rom 8:38; 1 Cor 15:24; Eph 1:21; Eph 3:10; Eph 6:11; Col 1:16; Col 2:10; Col 2:15
8. Archangels	Tobit; Dan 8-12; Lk 1:10-20, 26-38; 1 Thes 4:16; Jude 1:9
9. Angels	"Virtually every page of scripture speaks of angels" (St. Gregory the Great).

---

69 Parente, *The Angels*, 63-70.
70 See also, Dr. Mark Miravalle, *Time to Meet the Angels*; the excellent short article by Fr. Evaristus Eshiowu, *The Latin Mass* magazine, "The Forgotten Army", Spring 2000; and the Opus Angelorum website, www.opusangelorum.org.

The names of the first two choirs are Hebrew, while the other seven are from Greek or Latin.

But why call them "choirs"?

The term "choir" describes one of the primary functions of all angels: adoration. We recall the familiar scene in Lk 2:9-15 where "a multitude of the heavenly hosts" sings (or chants, as per the previous chapter) in praise of the newborn Messiah. People sing in choirs, so it was a small logical step to apply the term "choir" to groups of singing angels. Needless to say, artists throughout the centuries have loved the image.

The idea of "singing in ranks" also has a structural aspect to it that fits angelic organization. Think of an elaborate choral group like the Mormon Tabernacle Choir, where the various groups of singers stand in ranks when performing. The term "ranks" also suggests the appearance of an enormous pipe organ installed in the balcony of a Baroque church. Its pipes are arrayed in various ranks according to their sounds and sizes.

Who came up with the nine choirs idea?

The Church had formalized a theology of angelic choirs by the time of St. Ambrose (337-397 AD), but the theory achieved greater clarity and prominence from the writings of a mysterious theologian named Pseudo-Dionysius[71] (4th-5th century AD).

Of this theological giant we know virtually nothing. (Maybe he was really an angel in disguise.) However, he wrote a treatise on the nine choirs called *The Celestial Hierarchy* which became the authoritative work on angelic organization from that time forward. It's a marvelous work of subtle, lucid theology, which is still in print to this day.

Though not without its detractors in later centuries, Pseudo-Dionysius's description of the nine choirs became the gold standard for discussion of angelic organization. Other thinkers such as St. John

---

71 John Farina, ed. The Classics of Western Spirituality Series. *Pseudo Dionysius: The Complete Works*. New York: Paulist Press, 1987. Christian tradition holds that a man named Dionysius was the first Christian bishop of Athens. "Pseudo" is a prefix that designates someone who writes as him or in the tradition of his thought. See Bernard McGinn, et al., eds. *Angelic Spirituality: Medieval Perspectives on the Ways of Angels*. (Classics of Western Spirituality Series. Mahwah ,NJ: Paulist Press, 2002), xx.

Damascene, Peter Lombard, St. Thomas Aquinas and others repeated and augmented the theory. It has been passed down to our day with remarkable unanimity in Christian thought. Even Dante Alighieri included the nine choirs in his epic poem, *The Divine Comedy*, in the 14th century.

3. THE TWO GRADES

A question about St. Michael the Archangel immediately arises from these rankings.[72] How can the Prince of the Heavenly Host be a member of the *second lowest* rank of angels? Shouldn't St. Michael be considered the highest of all the angels?

This is a very good question and one that can be answered by appeal to the two grades theory,[73] which is another way of looking at angelic organization but which also doesn't contradict the nine choirs tradition. It implies that there are *two levels* of authority and power among the angels: archangel and angel. The Greek noun *arché*, used here as a prefix, means "ruler", "kingly", "magisterial", even "preeminent".[74] There are some angels who seem to be commanders of the angelic hosts.

Military orders are divided similarly between officers and enlisted men – those who command vs. those who carry out their commands. In a similar way, the angelic army is composed of the ruling and powerful angels who act as officers and the innumerable foot soldiers who execute their orders.

The two overlapping concepts of angel organization (nine choirs and two grades) explains why St. Michael can be seen both as a member of the second lowest rank of angels and as the five-star general of the entire force. According to this theory, St. Michael is a member of a lower order *by nature* but is the commander-in-chief of the angels *by grace*.

There is a traditional story which suggests that God gave St. Michael the premier place in heaven when Lucifer rebelled. Despite being of

---

72 He is called an "archangel" in Jud 9.
73 This term is the author's and is only a theological insight, not a matter of Catholic doctrine.
74 As per Strong's Greek concordance, cf. http://biblehub.com/greek/746.htm.

a lower rank and power than Lucifer (who tradition holds to be a Cherub or a Seraph), St. Michael was the first to rise from his place and rebuke Lucifer, who challenged God's sovereignty. It must have been a David and Goliath battle among angels.

There is a passage in Isaiah (14:13-14) that captures Lucifer's act of hubris. In it, the king of Babylon (a symbol of Satan) declares:

> I will scale the heavens;
> Above the stars of God I will set up my throne;
> …I will ascend above the tops of the clouds;
> I will be like the Most High!

The Hebrew name Michael means "Who-Is-Like-God". Grammatically, the compound word takes the form of a rhetorical question, along the lines of "Who would dare to compare himself to God?"

Michael's very name was a rebuke to Lucifer, who believed he could be "like the Most High". The theory is that God rewarded St. Michael for meritorious conduct[75] much the way a soldier would receive a medal of honor or a promotion in rank for heroism on the battlefield.

Are there other commanding angels? Judging from the evidence of scripture, there are many: the archangels Gabriel and Raphael, of course (in Daniel, Tobit, and Luke); the "seven spirits before God's throne" (Rev 1:4 and Tob 12:15); and the numerous "mighty" angels[76] in the Book of Revelation. Undoubtedly there are many more officers in the angelic army,[77] but God has not made them fully known to us. We will have to wait to meet them in the Kingdom.

4. (DIS)ORDER IN THE DEMONIC HORDE

Demons are also angels, albeit fallen ones, who at one time were members of the blessed angelic hierarchy. The Church affirms that the demons were created good in the beginning but fell into sin by their

---

75 Parente, *The Angels*, 84-85.
76 In Greek they are all called *ischus*, "mighty". Cf. Rev 5:2; Rev 10; Rev 18:21.
77 Other angels are distinguished by their mighty deeds: the angel who single-handedly vanquished 185,000 Assyrian soldiers (1 Kgs 19); the angel who announced the fall of Babylon (Rev 18:1-3); the angels of the Resurrection (Mt 28:2; 16:5; 24:4; Jn 20:12), etc. These too may be angelic officers.

own choice.[78] Some questions remain about their organization *after* they fell from grace. Did they retain their hierarchical structure or did they just fall into chaos? Is there still some order among the demons? These are fascinating questions.

Let's start with an affirmation by an authority in demonology, Fr. Gabriele Amorth, the former chief exorcist of the Diocese of Rome. In his incredible 1999 book, *An Exorcist Tells His Story*, Father noted that

> Satan was the brightest of the angels; he became the most evil of the devils and their chief. The demons remain bound to the same strict hierarchy that was given them when they were angels; principalities, thrones, dominions, and so on (Colossians 1:16). However, while the holy angels, whose chief is Michael, are bound by a hierarchy of love, the demons live under the rule of slavery.[79]

The idea that Satan went from the "brightest" of all the angels to the "most evil" after the fall is chilling in itself, but it indicates that some type of "inversion" took place. When the demons fell, their natural hierarchy remained but was turned on its head. The angels' hierarchy of love was replaced by a demonic social order that was a type of slavery, as Father Amorth noted. Now Satan rules from the bottom rather than from the top, and he rules his own demons with cruelty.[80]

So, there is order in the demonic horde because of their nature but disorder in their community due to their lack of grace. The demonic world must be in a state of perpetual war.

St. Thomas Aquinas affirms that the demons did not lose their natural angelic rankings when they fell. He says there are demonic Cherubim, demonic Virtues, demonic Principalities, etc. Members of these

---

78 As per the decree of the Second Council of Constantinople, referred to in Chapter 3.

79 Fr. Gabriele Amorth, *An Exorcist Tells His Story*, Nicoletta V. McKenzie, tr., San Francisco: Ignatius Press, 1999.

80 In his famous work *The Screwtape Letters*, C.S. Lewis facetiously calls this the "lowerarchy" of the demons. Also, Dante put Satan in the lowest point of hell, not the top, closest to the world of men.

orders retain their natural gifts[81] – which is why we ought to *prudently fear demons*.

St. Thomas doesn't believe that any angels fell from the ranks of the Seraphim, Thrones, or Dominions because these choirs are nowhere mentioned in scripture in association with the apostate angels or the works of evil.[82] Many theologians believe Lucifer was a Seraph, but Thomas believed he fell from the ranks of the Cherubim because of the extremely negative reference to an angel of that order in the Book of Ezekiel (28:14ff.).

To St. Thomas, angels of knowledge and wisdom have a greater tendency toward pride, which means that evil was much more likely to originate from the ranks of the angelic "intelligentsia" (Cherubim) than from the highest contemplative spirits (Seraphim). As someone who spent his whole life among scholars and intellectuals, St. Thomas probably had a point.

If there is any cooperation among demons, it's not because they love or respect one another. It's simply a matter of their common desire to destroy God's Kingdom and God's children. Their collaboration is sheer pragmatism as they make war on God and men. "The concord of demons," says St. Thomas,

> ...whereby some obey others, does not arise from mutual friendships, but from their common wickedness whereby they hate men, and fight against God's justice. For it belongs to wicked men to be joined to and subject to those whom they see to be stronger, in order to carry out their own wickedness.[83]

Evil men obey the commands of stronger evil men to achieve their goals. The same dynamic applies to demons.

But this raises another question: If the demons retain their natural

---

81 Aquinas, *Summa*, I.109.1.

82 The Virtues, Powers, and Principalities are cited by St. Paul in reference to demons in various passages of Romans, 1 Corinthians, Ephesians, and Colossians.

83 Aquinas, *Summa*, I.109.2 ad 2.

powers, then wouldn't a demonic Cherub or any high-ranking demon be stronger than a holy angel of lower rank? Thank God, this is not the case.

St. Thomas says that a holy angel of an inferior order is in no way subject to a more powerful demon of a higher rank because "the power of Divine justice to which the good angels cleave is stronger than the natural power of the demons."[84] So, even the lowest angels can defeat the strongest demons at any time by "the power of Divine justice" which they wield. Whew.

---

84 Ibid. I.109.4.ad 3. Another comment St. Thomas makes in I.112.1.ad 4 is insightful: "Every man or angel, insofar as he is united to God, becomes one spirit with God, and is thus superior to every other creature."

7

ANGELIC RELIGIOUS ORDERS

A priest friend of mine attended seminary in Rome and has an abundance of stories about the religious culture of the Eternal City. One of his most interesting stories involves the large lecture hall at the university that would slowly fill up with seminarians, priests, and nuns each day in preparation for class. Even the UN apparently is no match for the cultural diversity of an ecclesiastical university in Rome.

Father described a typical daily scene to me: The black-robed Benedictines were always the first to arrive, sitting there calmly while others milled around looking for places to sit. Franciscans wandered in at intervals, wearing their various black, brown, and grey habits. The Dominicans usually entered with a splash, attired in their white tunics and black capes. These men came from a hundred countries around the globe, giving a human face to the universal Church.

The religious sisters were even more diverse in their habits and cultures. The nuns from Africa and Asia were the stars of the show: their habits were white, pale blue, shocking blue, green, yellow, red, and even pink!

We could get caught up in the fascinating garments and miss the most important element of religious life, however. These communities are called religious "orders" for a reason. They are *ordered* or organized for a mission, the Church's mission.

Angels have a diversity of identities and missions too, so it only makes sense that they could be organized into "religious orders" of angels, metaphorically speaking. It's a radical thesis, I know, and it's not doctrine as such, but it's an intriguing idea. Let's explore some further ideas about angel organization to see if the idea holds up to scrutiny.

1. THE THREE HIERARCHIES

Pseudo-Dionysius, from the last chapter, showed his true genius when he further divided the nine choirs into three hierarchies. He used the biblical symbol for divine perfection (the number three) to organize three divisions of three choirs each as a way to reflect the inner life of the Holy Trinity.

These three-fold divisions he called "hierarchies", which in Greek means "the rule of priests" or "the rule of holy ones".

A hierarchy, he explains, is a structure (in this case spiritual) that lifts everything in creation and every individual soul *upward* to God, much the way a chain of workers passes things from one person to another to move things to their goal, or the way an elevator carries its passengers upward to their destinations. An angelic hierarchy is a living structure of spiritual beings working together that increases their overall power to implement God's will in the universe.

Pseudo-Dionysius calls it a "perfect arrangement" for bringing both angels and humans into union with God:

> For every member of the hierarchy, perfection consists in this, that it is uplifted to imitate God as far as possible and, more wonderful still, that it becomes…a reflection of the workings of God…. Each will actually imitate God in the way suitable to whatever role it has.[85]

In other words, the three-three pattern of angelic hierarchies explains how angels participate in and hand on the divine life to others. The following chart[86] spells out this "perfect arrangement":

---

85 Farina, *Pseudo Dionysius*, 154.
86 Eshiowu, "The Forgotten Army", 41-42. Fr. Eshiowu cites another author, Doyle Gilligan (*Devotion to the Holy Angels*), for this insight.

| THREE ANGELIC HIERARCHIES |||
Description	Choirs	Function
Top Hierarchy		
Contemplative	Seraphim-Cherubim-Thrones	Worship God directly
Middle Hierarchy		
Regulative	Dominations-Virtues-Powers	Preside over the good order of the universe
Lower Hierarchy		
Administrative	Principalities-Archangels-Angels	Act as monitors over the world and affairs of men

This is the clearest explanation of why the nine choirs are divided into three sets of three. Angels have big jobs.

What do hierarchies actually do? Pseudo-Dionysus, not surprisingly, gives them exactly three functions. Hierarchies purify, enlighten, and sanctify – very angelic works.

Pseudo-Dionysius was really on to something. All angels participate in some way in the three-fold work of purifying us of sin, enlightening our darkened minds, and raising our souls up to union with God.[87] The seven angelic ministries we spoke about in Chapter 1 are all variations of these spiritual works.

2. THE THREE REALMS

Hinted at in the chart above are the "places" where the angels carry out their works of purifying, enlightening, and unifying. God's drama of salvation encompasses the totality of the created universe – visible and invisible – the various realms of which are placed under the authority of angels. Because of its three-fold structure, you might think that this theory comes from Pseudo-Dionysius, but it comes from scripture itself.

---

87 Danielou, *Angels and Their Mission*, 85.

In the bible, the created world consists of three spheres: heaven (God's home), mid-heaven (the physical universe, sometimes described as "the air" or "atmosphere" or generically as "the heavens"), and earth (land, sea, sometimes including the region described as "under the earth" or "Sheol").

The above three terms are used most strikingly in the Book of Revelation,[88] where the action surrounding the end times unfolds in these three realms. They are *spheres of influence and authority* rather than physical areas. (It would be incorrect, for example, to understand heaven as a physical place.)

The angels operate naturally in these distinct realms because each one is assigned to his own place by God. They exercise their power and authority much the same way that earthly authorities exercise their respective powers at local, national, and regional levels.

Let's look at some scriptural evidence of angelic operations in these realms.

Heaven

The top angelic hierarchy is responsible for the realm of heaven and the direct service of God. Various biblical passages bear witness to this: Isaiah sees the Seraphim in the throne room of God (Is 6) and Ezekiel has visions of the Cherubim serving God's heavenly Temple (Ez 1).[89] The very name "Thrones" reflects God's symbol of authority in heaven (Rev 4 and 5; 20:11-12). We only see these types of angels in heaven or related to Temple worship in some way.

Mid-Heaven

The Dominations-Virtues-Powers have authority over the universe and all its elements. This concept is wonderfully expressed in certain passages of Revelation which depict angels from this hierarchy as standing on the globe or the sun and ruling over the atmosphere. The

---

[88] The Greek terms in Revelation are "heaven" (*ho ouranos*), "mid-heaven" (*ho mesouranos*), and "earth" (*he gey*).

[89] See Ezekiel chapters 1 and 10 as well as Ex 25:18-22 and 2 Chr 3:10-13, where the Cherubim are fixtures of the Ark of the Covenant and Mercy Seat.

glorious angel that issues the condemnation of Babylon, for example, could be an angel from this middle hierarchy: he pronounces his judgment from the air (i.e., mid-heaven). He also wields enormous power over the entire world: "Having great authority," says the passage, "the earth became illumined by his splendor" (Rev 18:1). He is also an angel of judgment, consistent with the strength and authority bestowed upon angels of this hierarchy.[90]

World

The lowest of the three hierarchies is that of the Principalities-Archangels-Angels, who are given authority over the earth and the affairs of men. We generally see these types of angels in scripture when they act upon the world. An angel in Chapter 18 of Revelation, for example, calls out to *the nations of the earth* in urgent terms, warning them of the dangers of association with the evil harlot: "Depart from her, my people, so as not to take part in her sins and receive a share in her plagues…" (Rev 18:4-5). Given his concern for nations, even calling them "my people", this angel is probably a Principality.

As for the archangels and angels, there is abundant evidence in the bible of their authority over the world of men. Below is another chart which focuses on the three realms. It includes a fourth angel grouping not explored yet in any detail: the demons.

---

90 See Appendix 2 for a description of the various functions of angels in their respective choirs.

NATURES OF FIRE

THE THREE REALMS	
Choirs	Realm
Top Hierarchy	
Seraphim-Cherubim-Thrones	Heaven: God's Temple and Throne
Middle Hierarchy	
Dominations-Virtues-Powers	Mid-Heaven: the universe, the sky, "the heavens" or "the air"
Lower Hierarchy	
Principalities-Archangels-Angels	World: earth, sea, land, affairs of men
Demonic Horde	
All demonic choirs / orders	Mid-heaven, the World, (ultimately) Hell

Some think the proper realm of the fallen angels is hell, but that will not be entirely true until the end of time. Michael cast the apostate angels down to *earth* when they rebelled. Revelation 12 refers to the dragon's tail sweeping "a third of the stars from the sky and [hurling] them down to the earth" (Rev 12:4), a clear reference to the number of angels who followed Satan's lead. In other words, there are no fallen angels in the realm of heaven.

A later verse in that chapter describes the demons' *realm of action*: "But woe to you, earth and sea, for the Devil has come down to you in great fury" (Rev 12:12). We can add "air" (mid-heaven) to this list because, according to St. Paul, evil spirits operate "in the heavens" (Eph 6:12) and Satan is "the ruler of the power of the air, the spirit that is now at work in the disobedient" (Eph 2:2).

So, basically, evil spirits are everywhere in the created world. Lucky us.

But while God allows demons to roam the earth now (Job 1:7), eventually all damned spirits and souls will be locked away for all eternity in *their own realm*, which will be what we commonly understand as the hell of the damned. Prior to that, the realm of Satan and his band of fallen angels is the sky above us, the world around us, and especially the battlefield of our own souls, as St. Padre Pio often taught.

3. ANGELIC RELIGIOUS ORDERS

As I said in the introduction to this chapter, it's not hard to notice that the angelic groupings bear a certain similarity to religious orders in the Church, but angels were at this ordering business long before the Church was even born.

St. Thomas Aquinas always used the term "order", not "choir", to describe angel rankings.[91] He was using a theological term that has a very wide range of related meanings in church usage: ordination, holy orders, religious orders, canonical orders, the ordo (a liturgical calendar), and Ordinary (a term used to describe a diocesan bishop and a liturgical season), among others. In a similar sense, the medical profession uses the term "orderly" to designate non-medical professionals who perform helpful services in the care of the sick. All of these uses of the word "order" derive from the same generic Latin root, "ordo".[92]

If we view angelic choirs metaphorically as nine distinct angelic *religious orders*, we may be surprised how well the analogy fits. Church religious orders have numerous characteristics of organization and structure in common with the ranks of angels:

- Religious orders have "founders" (analogous to the first and highest members of the angelic choirs);

- They are arranged in hierarchies of authority;

- Their members are consecrated, i.e., take holy vows;

- Each religious order has its own unique mission (though

---

91 Aquinas, *Summa*, I.108-109.
92 The term "order" in Notre Dame's online *Latin Dictionary and Grammar Aid*: "ordo -inis m. [a series, line, row, order]; milit. [a line, rank, file]; 'ordinem ducere', [to be a centurion]; polit. and socially, [an order, rank, class]; in gen. [order, arrangement]; 'ordine', [in turn, in due order, regularly]; 'extra ordinem', [in an unusual, irregular manner]", http://www.archives.nd.edu/cgi-bin/lookup.pl?stem=Ordo, accessed 8/3/20.

some orders overlap in mission areas and functions with others);

- They have distinct charisms (spiritual gifts) that inspire and drive their work;
- They have unique religious habits that identify their members (analogous to the angelic designs and architecture we spoke of in Chapter 4).

Finally, many of these orders are, or can be, militaristic in their mission of defending the Church, like the angels.

Another curious parallel is that the three main families of religious orders correspond to the three modes of angelic ministries and their realms:

ANGEL HIERARCHIES / RELIGIOUS ORDERS PARALLELS				
Angels	Church	Realm	Ministry	Examples
Contemplative	Contemplative Orders	Heaven	Prayer, Penance, Adoration	Benedictines, Carthusians
Regulative	Missionary and Teaching Orders	Universe	Education, Evangelization	Jesuits, Franciscans, Dominicans
Administrative	Service Orders	World	Salvation of souls, Works of mercy	Missionaries of Charity, Good Shepherd Sisters

Religious orders also seem to reflect the three angelic ministries: some orders are dedicated to the mission of *purification* (penitential and service orders), others to *enlightenment* (educational orders), still others to *union* (contemplative orders).

Most importantly, the overall goal of a religious order is the perfection of its members. Pseudo-Dionysius's theory is that the angels themselves, as sinless and full of goodness as they are, still participate in the ongoing process of attaining perfect holiness in Christ.

Thus, we can see many parallels to our Church's religious orders reflected in the life of the angels – and vice versa. Whether or not individual members of religious orders *act* like angels is quite another matter.

8

AWESOME ANGELS

If there were such a thing as an Angelic Hall of Fame, the angels in the next two chapters would be in it. These angels are easy to gloss over in a cursory reading of scripture, but a deeper reflection on them gives one the feeling of – there is no better word – awe.

Angels are awe-inspiring beings whose witness in the pages of scripture reveals a mere spark of their glory. But as limited as our perceptions of the spiritual world may be, God wants us to know and love the angels, so it's worth taking the time to get to know a few of them in more detail.

Biblical authors try their very best to describe the beauty and grandeur of angels, but their human words inevitably fall short of capturing the full reality. Most of the people in the bible who had direct contact with angels were rendered mute or thrown into abject terror by the experience of angelic splendor.

The prophet Ezekiel, for example, saw the Cherubim coming toward him in a vision during the Babylonian exile, and all he could say was, "It was awesome" (Ez 1:22)![93] The soldiers at Jesus' tomb on the day of the Resurrection "became like dead men" when an angel in blazing robes descended from heaven to roll the stone away (Mt 28:2-4).

---

93 For a full account of Ezekiel's visions, kindly see the article "The Power and the Glory of Ezekiel's Cherubim", at the author's *Sacred Windows* website (www.sacredwindows.com).

Scripture offers so many astounding accounts of angels that it would be hard to describe even a portion of them in a small book, but I want to introduce you to a few Angel Hall of Famers in the limited space we have. Note that the titles below are not personal names (as per the prohibition of naming in Chapter 3). The titles describe their missions or functions in the biblical passages. Perhaps we'll learn their real names when we meet them in heaven.

1. ELIJAH'S CHARIOTS OF FIRE

We know from the Second Book of Kings that God took the prophet Elijah to heaven *alive* in a most dramatic way. Noah's grandfather, the ancient patriarch Enoch, is the only other person in the Old Testament who went to heaven without dying (cf. Gen 5:24; Heb 11:5).

Elijah's prophetic powers were so vast that a constant Hebrew tradition predicted that he would come back in person to prepare Israel for the Messiah.[94] Elijah was the epitome of the prophet: he rebuked kings and queens; he slew false prophets; by his command he stopped the heavens from giving rain; he even exercised authority over life and death several times. Elijah is prophetic power and divine purpose all rolled into one fiery saint.

It is no wonder that angels of fire are associated with him; fire seemed to accompany Elijah everywhere he went.[95] In a fitting departure from this earth, God sent angels in the form of blazing horses and chariots to gather him up and bring him to heaven.

Although the motif of fiery beings scooping humans from the earth and escorting them to the gods is a fairly common one in world mythology, it's reasonable to assume that these horses and chariots were more than metaphorical. Elijah did indeed disappear from earth, so the event was not merely symbolic, and some type of living creatures

---

[94] Jesus made mention of this tradition (Mt 17:12), proving that it was well-established even in His day. In fact, Jewish tradition still predicts this: Jewish families set a place for Elijah at their Passover tables every year in the hopes that it will be the year he comes back as a herald of the Messiah.

[95] Fire leapt upon and consumed the sacrifice he offered in the face of the prophets of Baal (1 Kgs 18:38); there was fire on Mt. Horeb (1 Kgs 19:23); he called down fire from heaven to consume fifty soldiers representing the apostate king of Israel (2 Kgs 1:9-12).

carried him away. If these metaphorical "horses and chariots" were not angels, it would be hard to determine what they were.

The story of the prophet's departure is short but full of high intensity and wonder. The setting shows that Elijah and his apprentice, Elisha, have re-traced the steps of God's people – from Gilgal (the first place of worship in the Promised Land, north of Jericho) to the Jordan – returning to the harsh desert circumstances where their people first experienced God. Here, the prophets experience divine power in a new way.

The fiery angels' appearance became a doorway between worlds for Elijah and an entryway into a new life for Elisha. Before the angels arrive, the younger prophet asks for a spiritual gift – "a double portion" of Elijah's spirit. Then:

> As they walked on still conversing, a fiery chariot and fiery horses came between the two of them, and Elijah went up to heaven in a whirlwind, and Elisha saw it happen. He cried out, "My father! my father! Israel's chariot and steeds!" Then he saw him no longer (2 Kgs 2:11-12a).

We get the impression from this scene that fire entirely envelops the two men. It is described as a "whirlwind", a sort of fiery tornado or vortex of flames. The blazing chariot and horses pass *between* them, yet no one is burned.

How is that possible? "It is not earthly fire, which would simply burn them up," notes Judith Lang. "The chariots and horses that drive between" the two men "are *made of* fire".[96] It is spiritual fire that will not harm, but only purify, a human soul. We can see in our mind's eye Elijah swept up in the hurricane force of the firestorm and riding into the heavens with flowing beard and robes erupting in flames of glory. Hollywood films are no match for God's drama.

Of these raucous horses and chariots alive with heavenly fire we are given no further details. They are part of a mystical experience whose flames serve a definite purpose. As earthly fire rises, so chariots of fire

---

96 Lang, *Angels of God*, 34. Emphasis mine.

rise in one direction: heavenward. "Angels are figures of their very function, which is to cross over, to move between earth and heaven. They are both the door and what comes through it".[97]

The angels bridge the divide between heaven and earth in order to retrieve the prophet who had raised up so many men of earth to heaven. Then, as the doorway to heaven for one prophet closes, the entryway for another prophet is thrown wide open. Elisha may now return to the community of men as a prophet in his own right after having been purified in heart and soul by angels of fire.

The new seer is granted his wish to be a prophet with a "double portion" of Elijah's spirit. Taking up the prophetic mantle now, he strikes the water and crosses back over the Jordan River (2 Kgs 2:12b-14) to bring the divine fire once again to men.

2. ST. PETER'S GUARDIAN ANGEL

Someone once quipped that a guardian angel's dream job was to be assigned to guard the pope. As of this writing, we can say with certainty that there have been 266 angels who have been so blessed, starting with the one we were told about in the Acts of the Apostles: the guardian angel of the *first* pope.

The incident regarding Peter's guardian angel is unique. This is the only time in the bible where a personal guardian angel is directly identified as such. St. Peter met his own guardian angel face to face in the bowels of a prison.

The setting of this angelic encounter is the persecution launched by Herod Antipas in Palestine shortly after the day of Pentecost. Herod beheaded James, the brother of John, and then went after Peter. When Herod threw him into prison under heavy guard, the Church members prayed to God for their leader (Acts 12:1-5).

Note the key element here: *the Church's prayer*. It is always in an atmosphere of prayer, penance, and dependence upon God that angels do their best work. The details of the story show how drastic the situation was for Peter:

---

97 Ibid.

On the very night before Herod was to bring him to trial, Peter, secured by double chains, was sleeping between two soldiers, while outside the door guards kept watch on the prison. Suddenly the angel of the LORD stood by him and a light shone in the cell. He tapped Peter on the side and awakened him, saying, "Get up quickly." The chains fell from his wrists. The angel said to him, "Put on your belt and your sandals." He did so. Then he said to him, "Put on your cloak and follow me." So he followed him out, not realizing that what was happening through the angel was real; he thought he was seeing a vision. They passed the first guard, then the second, and came to the iron gate leading out to the city, which opened for them by itself. They emerged and made their way down an alley, and suddenly the angel left him. Then Peter recovered his senses and said, "Now I know for certain that [the] LORD sent his angel and rescued me from the hand of Herod and from all that the Jewish people had been expecting" (Acts 12:6-11).

This story has all the hallmarks of a dramatic angel rescue. First, the angel saves Peter in the nick of time (his execution was only a few hours away). Second, the angel acts with military precision, giving three short commands in quick succession so that nothing could possibly be misunderstood by the sleepy Peter. Third, iron chains, barriers, locks, gates, etc. melt away at the silent command of the heavenly visitor, illustrating the kind of immediate power angels have over the elements of the material world.

Finally, and most importantly, after freeing Peter, the angel sent him out to continue the Church's mission of spreading the gospel. Peter makes a beeline to the house where the early Church is gathered to pray for him, but the maid who heard Peter's voice forgets to let him in! In her excitement, she runs to tell the group that he is standing at the door, and they can't believe it is Peter. They think it is his *guardian angel* (Acts 12:11-18).

This comical incident shows the Church's acknowledgement that their leader was rescued by an angel. Peter himself told them to share the good news of his rescue, which must have been an extremely consoling message for those who were in the grip of a fierce persecution.

As for the Church's first persecutor, Herod Antipas, the angel had other plans for him:

> Herod, attired in royal robes, and seated on the rostrum, addressed them publicly. The assembled crowd cried out, "This is the voice of a god, not of a man." At once the angel of the LORD struck him down because he did not ascribe the honor to God, and he was eaten by worms and breathed his last (Acts 12:19-23).

As if to underline the point that the evil actions of men do not inhibit the work of the Church, the passage ends with a very angelic message: "But the word of God continued to spread and grow" (Acts 12:24).

3. HERALD OF THE END TIME

The Book of Revelation contains some of the most stunning images of angels in the bible. Of the uncountable hosts of angels that appear in Revelation, the Herald of the End Time is easily the most riveting.[98] Take some time to meditate on this angel's appearance and message: he is sent by God to announce *the end of time itself*. Imagine that.

This angel delivers the very last word of warning to humanity before God ends it all. The angel bellows that "there shall be no more delay" (Rev 10:6). The original Greek sentence could also be rendered more colloquially: "Time has run out".[99] Here is how Revelation describes him:

---

98 Here I am making the distinction that Judith Lang points out in her perceptive book, *The Angels of God: Understanding the Bible* (93-94): a herald is one who comes strictly to deliver a message with little or no interaction with the recipients of the message. Messengers, envoys, and ambassadors, on the other hand, engage in dialogue with the receivers, which is how most angels interact with humans in the bible. But the Herald of the End Times is not a simple guardian angel.

99 A literal translation from the Greek is "Time no longer shall be" (χρόνος οὐκέτι ἔσται,). What looks like a comma at the end of the Greek phrase is actually the Greek form of the exclamation mark (!) which occurs rarely in the New Testament but here serves to emphasize the urgency of the message. Χρόνος (chronos) is the Greek word and root for the English word "chronological"; in other words, human time.

> Then I saw another mighty angel come down from heaven wrapped in a cloud, with a halo around his head; his face was like the sun and his feet were like pillars of fire. In his hand he held a small scroll that had been opened. He placed his right foot on the sea and his left foot on the land, and then he cried out in a loud voice as a lion roars. When he cried out, the seven thunders raised their voices, too.... (Rev 10:1-4).

It is both breathtaking and frightening to realize that each one of us will hear that commanding voice one day.

The Herald of the End Time bristles with authority. He came "from heaven" and wears a visible halo about his head, symbolizing his radiant holiness. He is called "mighty", a Greek term (*ischus*) that is used to describe only three angels in the bible who carry out the most solemn missions.

This angel exudes the radiant glory and power of God in his countenance and bearing. True to his angelic nature, he is a messenger of grace and fire: his face is "like the sun", a fiery star, and his feet (or legs) are made of fire. No one has ever seen anything like this on earth. Here is an angel of immense glory breaking into human history to announce the end of all things.

This mighty angel gives the impression that he is *Jesus Christ's personal envoy*,[100] sent to deliver the Lord's final warning to sinful man. And what an announcement!

> Then the angel I saw standing on the sea and on the land raised his right hand to heaven and swore by the one who lives forever and ever, who created heaven and earth and sea and all that is in them, "There shall be no more delay. At the time when you hear the seventh angel blow his trumpet, the mysterious plan of God shall be fulfilled, as he promised to his servants the prophets" (Rev 10:5-7).

---

[100] Jesus is described in similar imagery in Revelation 1:13-16, particularly, "His face shone like the sun at its brightest" (16).

When we read that the angel places one foot on the land and the other on the sea, we should not think in terms of *physical* size, which does not apply to angels. He is not some kind of ancient titan LORDing his authority over others; he is a powerful spiritual messenger of Almighty God.

Planting himself on land and sea indicates his spiritual authority over the earth and over mankind, much as a conquering warrior would straddle an enemy he has just subdued. This divine messenger stands above a world full of sinners to announce the urgency of repentance.

The angel does not just show up and blurt out a message like a town crier of old. His movements are staged and deliberate to create an effect: he first descends from heaven "wrapped in a cloud" and plants himself on earth and sea with feet "like pillars of fire" (Rev. 10:1-2), with a firm grasp on his authority. He mirrors the angel who went before God's people when they left Egypt. That angel appeared both as a "pillar of fire" at night and "pillar of cloud" during the day (Ex 14 and 23), echoing perfectly the description of the Herald of the End Time.

Then, in a dramatic gesture, the angel *roars like a lion* to get the attention of the entire world! His is a voice and a message that no human being can possibly ignore.

Finally, he raises his hand to heaven, invoking the most solemn gesture of truth-telling known to man. He *swears an oath* to confirm that his authority derives from the highest possible source: "the one who lives forever and ever, who created heaven and earth and sea and all that is in them".

His message echoes the words of our crucified Savior: "It is finished" (Jn 19:30). What, specifically, is finished? Chronological time. The world as we know it. Sin.

No one trifles with a being like this.

The Herald of the End Time is truly one of the most glorious angels in the entire bible, and the last angelic voice humanity will hear before the world comes to an end. The question each of us much ask ourselves is this: when that voice rings out over heaven and earth, *will I be ready*?

HONORABLE MENTIONS

The mighty messengers in this chapter are not the only awesome angels of God to grace the pages of scripture. Certain others deserve honorable mentions. We could easily add the following angels to the list, some of whom we've mentioned already:

- The Cherub of fire who was placed at the entrance to the Garden of Eden (Gen 3);

- The angel who saved Isaac from execution in the nick of time (Gen 22);

- The angel who wrestled with Jacob (Gen 32);

- The angel who sent Gideon to save the Israelites (Jdg 6);

- The five majestic angels "riding on golden-bridled horses" leading the Maccabees into battle (2 Macc 10);

- The panoply of angels in the Book of the Prophet Zechariah (Zech 1-5);

- The angel who appeared to St. Joseph directing him to protect the Baby Jesus and Our Lady (Mt 1-2);

- The angels of the harvest at the end of time (Mt 13 and Rev 14);

- The angels who appeared to the shepherds in Bethlehem (Lk 2);

- The angel who strengthened Jesus in the Garden of Gethsemane (Lk 22);

- The angel who opened the gates of the jail and instructed the Apostles to return to preaching (Acts 5);

- The angel who assisted Philip in baptizing the Ethiopian eunuch (Acts 8);

- The angel who brought Peter and Cornelius together (Acts 10);
- The angel who saved Paul and his companions from shipwreck (Acts 27).

Lastly, the Book of Revelation seems like it has a whole gallery of awesome ministering angels – avengers, messengers, incense angels, servants of the Temple, even exorcist angels – but their stories will have to wait for another book!

9

AVENGING ANGELS

Now we've arrived at the most unexpected and seemingly incongruous role the holy angels have ever played: that of executioners. *Do angels actually kill people?* you might ask. The answer to this question is as simple as it is unexpected: if God wants them to, yes, angels kill people. These are angels you will not find on holy cards.

Some angels are executors of God's judgment, instruments of His power, and avengers of true Justice. Even if you haven't previously noticed them playing this role, there is plenty of biblical evidence that angels carry out these drastic functions. Remember the angel that struck down Herod in the last chapter?

The most obvious examples of avenging angels in scripture are the two angels who dealt rather rudely with Sodom and Gomorrah (Gen 19) and the angel known as "the destroyer" (called that in Ex 12:23) who "executed judgment on all the gods of Egypt" (Ex 12:12). Oh, and don't forget that mysterious "band of destroying angels" spoken of in the psalms (Ps 78:49) or the little matter of those Four Horsemen of the Apocalypse.

Vanquishing corruption, bringing down God's judgment on unrepentant idolatry, dispatching the wicked – yes, angels kill people

– usually bad people.[101] There is no angel explicitly called "the angel of death" in scripture[102] because a destroying angel simply carries out a mission. No holy angel personally represents death, which the Book of Wisdom says entered the world "by the envy of the devil" (Wis 2:24). The avenging angels represent *God's implacable authority over life and death*.

Angel warriors are the most recognizable executors of judgment in scripture. Yet, while all warfare involves death, spiritual warriors do much more than kill. They are involved in the struggles of God's people. They strategize, fight, protect, and guide others away from danger.

In that respect, let's begin with a story that features the greatest of all warrior angels: Michael.

1. JOSHUA'S COMMANDER

Warfare is an angel's natural inclination. Angels were summoned to violent spiritual combat before human time began (see Rev 12). This is not human warfare as such, although humans can be dragged into it in many ways. It is war involving the conflict of angelic wills and intelligences. If you wonder how mind and will – spiritual faculties – can be "violent", simply listen to the lies, deceptions, and character assassinations of the modern media. That kind of thing is spiritual warfare, and it goes on all around us every day.

It's not at all surprising, then, to find that the angels are constantly giving advice to men about how to conduct human wars. They also *participate in* human conflicts in tangible ways (on behalf of Gideon, Elijah, Hezekiah, and the Maccabees, for example).

A remarkable account of an angelic intervention in battle occurred when Joshua and the Israelites entered the Promised Land and besieged the city of Jericho. As they camped before the city, they awaited further word about what to do with Jericho. Would the people of Jericho

---

101 But not exclusively. The first born children of the Egyptians were not evil, of course, nor were the thousands of innocent Israelites who were killed as a punishment for King David's sin of census-taking (2 Sam 24:15-16).

102 See www.compellingtruth.org/angel-of-death.html, "Does an angel of death exist?", accessed 10/19/20.

surrender? Would they fight? Would the siege be lifted or stall indefinitely? The dramatic tension in the story is high.

As if seeking answers to these unspoken questions, Joshua retreats to high ground above the city, looking down at it, and has a vision of a mighty angel that momentarily stuns him: he sees a mysterious being dressed for war and brandishing a sword.

Before he realizes who this warrior is, Joshua, the great commander of God's people, orders the "man" to identify himself, only to find that he himself is the one being ordered. Recall from Chapter 5 that angels most often speak to men in commands, not pious words.

True to form, the angel identifies himself – "I am the commander of the army of the LORD" – and then issues his own command to Joshua: "Remove your sandals from your feet, for the place on which you are standing is holy." Joshua immediately complies (Josh 5:13-15).

Here we see the clear pattern of human encounters with angels. Men fall to the ground in awe or terror when confronted with unearthly holiness. The angel sanctified the ground by his presence and then told Joshua to remove his sandals before the LORD, reminiscent of Joshua's own predecessor, Moses, standing before the burning bush (Ex 3).

"The earth upon which the vision takes place, where the angel figure is made visible," says Judith Lang, "becomes a threshold of heaven."[103] Joshua is standing at a doorway between heaven and earth, an opening created by the presence of the warrior messenger.

It isn't difficult to know the identity of the angel who reveals himself here as "the commander of the army of the LORD".[104] This can be none other than the Prince of the Heavenly Host, St. Michael the Archangel. In this scene, we are witnessing a dramatic *contrast of natures*. There is a proper order here: the glorious commander of the angelic army of God towers over the prostrate commander of Israel's human army.

The angel delivers a message that is a model of military precision,

---

103 Lang, *Angels of God*, 31.

104 The only incidents in the bible where angels reveal their names involve the holy archangels: Gabriel (Dan 8:16 and Lk 1:19) and Raphael (Tob 12:15) reveal their own names. Michael's name is revealed too, although he does not speak his own name but leaves it to the testimony of others (Dan 10:13; Jud 9; Rev 12:7).

spoken in the clipped speech of a command personality. Here it is the LORD Himself who seems to speak *through* the angel:[105]

> I have delivered Jericho, its king, and its warriors into your power. Have all the soldiers circle the city, marching once around it. Do this for six days, with seven priests carrying ram's horns ahead of the ark. On the seventh day march around the city seven times, and have the priests blow the horns. When they give a long blast on the ram's horns and you hear the sound of the horn, all the people shall shout aloud. The wall of the city will collapse, and the people shall attack straight ahead. (Josh 6:1-5)

Notice that Michael starts by announcing the final outcome of the battle – the enemy has *already* been delivered into their hands. This is a word out of time. The only thing lacking is the implementation of the plan in the course of human time, which is why Michael comes to announce a battle plan.

St. Michael's Jericho plan is full of symbolism and power. Seven is a perfect number in the bible, symbolizing the completeness of the divine plan. There are

- Seven priests;
- Seven days marching around the city;
- On the seventh day,
- They march seven times around the enemy bastion.

Furthermore, this battle has a sacred character: consecrated priests carry the Ark of the Covenant, the holy of holies, as they march and blow rams' horns.

The type of horn they blew, the shofar, inaugurates the Jewish New

---

105 In many Old Testament passages, the angel who appears acts as an entry point to a direct encounter with the Lord Himself. In these cases, he is usually called "The Angel of the Lord" (cf. Gen 16:7-12; 21:17-18; 22:11-18; Ex 3:2; Jdg 2:1-4; 5:23; 6:11-24; 13:3-22; 2 Sam 24:16; Zech 1:12; 3:1; 12:8), as we noted in the Introduction.

Year (Rosh Hashana) and Day of Atonement (Yom Kippur) each year, among other uses. Oddly enough, it is also used in Jewish exorcisms, which, in a way, symbolized that this battle would be a spiritual victory over all forces that oppose God's will, represented here by the pagan people to be conquered.

It is not with military weapons but with their voices of prayer and praise that the people directly engage the battle: they must shout! Never in the history of warfare have *sound waves* won a military victory. Yet this was God's plan, and the angel marshals divine force to achieve its effect.

True to Michael's prophecy, the wall of Jericho collapses at the united voices of God's people: "As the horns blew, the people began to shout.... The wall collapsed, and the people attacked the city straight ahead and took it" (Josh 6:20).

The major take-away lesson from Joshua's commander must be this: angels help us win victories over both spiritual and temporal evils.

2. BANE OF THE ASSYRIANS

The most astonishing biblical example of an avenging angel is found in the Second Book of Kings. The King of Assyria, Sennacherib, and his army laid siege to Jerusalem,[106] which caused the faithful King Hezekiah to shake in mortal anguish. The Assyrian king's overwhelming arrogance, however, was the decisive factor in the contest, as we shall see.

Sennacherib sent his envoys to taunt Hezekiah to his face and to blaspheme Israel's God, Yahweh. Here is the message – dripping with arrogance – that the envoys delivered to King Hezekiah on behalf of the Assyrian king:

> Thus shall you say to Hezekiah, king of Judah: "Do not let your God in whom you trust deceive you by saying, 'Jerusalem will not be handed over to the king of Assyria.' You, certainly, have heard what the kings of Assyria have done to all the lands: they put them under the ban! And are you to

---

106 This historical event occurred in 701 BC.

be rescued? Did the gods of the nations whom my fathers destroyed deliver them…?'" (2 Kgs 19:10-13)

It is not wise to taunt God. Sennacherib would eventually have to eat his words.

The good King Hezekiah's first instinct was to go directly to the Temple, prostrate himself before the Lord, and ask for protection in the face of this mortal threat. He must have been a truly holy man because his prayer was perfect, balancing the realism of the threat with Israel's ancient trust in their God. His beautiful prayer is worth repeating in full:

> Lord, God of Israel, enthroned on the cherubim! You alone are God over all the kingdoms of the earth. It is you who made the heavens and the earth. Incline your ear, Lord, and listen! Open your eyes, Lord, and see! Hear the words Sennacherib has sent to taunt the living God. Truly, O Lord, the kings of Assyria have laid waste the nations and their lands. They gave their gods to the fire—they were not gods at all, but the work of human hands—wood and stone, they destroyed them. Therefore, Lord, our God, save us from this man's power, that all the kingdoms of the earth may know that you alone, Lord, are God. (2 Kgs 19:15-19)

Hezekiah had hardly finished uttering his prayer when the prophet Isaiah carried Yahweh's long and quite poetic response to the king, which is one of the greatest "reverse taunts" in history (2 Kgs 19:21-34), ending with the words, "I will shield and save this city for my own sake and for the sake of David my servant."

Sennacherib was in for a big surprise. In fact, Isaiah's prophecy was fulfilled that very night by an avenging angel:

> That night the angel of the Lord went forth and struck down one hundred and eighty-five thousand men in the Assyrian camp. Early the next morning, there they were,

dead, all those corpses! So Sennacherib, the king of Assyria, broke camp, departed, returned home, and stayed in Nineveh (2 Kgs 19:35-36).

Such carnage wrought by one angel – 185,000 dead Assyrians! Scripture does not describe the mighty angel who did this. It just gives us an indication of his power by showing us the outcome of his action.

As for the arrogant Sennacherib, he didn't fare so well either, but his punishment was more along the lines of human justice: "When he was worshiping in the temple of his god Nisroch, his sons Adrammelech and Sharezer struck him down with the sword and fled into the land of Ararat. His son Esarhaddon reigned in his place" (2 Kgs 19:37).

So astonished were the Israelites by the power of Assyria's Bane that at least three other biblical books mention the event (Tob 1:21; Sir 48:24, and Is 37:36), two of them centuries after the fact. There are even two secular historians of the ancient world, Flavius Josephus and Herodotus, who refer to the angel's astounding act of vengeance on behalf of God's people.[107]

As I said, it is not wise to blaspheme the living God.

3. PROTECTORS OF THE TEMPLE

The historical books of the Old Testament lead chronologically to the brink of the New Testament, and angels accompany them all the way. Some of these books contain marvelous depictions of spiritual and actual warfare.

The Second Book of Maccabees, in particular, shows angels coming to the aid of Israel's warriors in remarkable ways. Chapters 3, 5, 10, and 11 of this book tell tales of angelic interventions on behalf of the Maccabees (a priestly/kingly dynasty of the Jews), but the tales are too long to recount here. We can only focus on the single incident in 2 Maccabees 3 which shows angels as protectors of the Temple of the LORD. To fully appreciate the story, we first need some historical background.[108]

A wicked Jewish priest, Simon, betrays his people by reporting to

---

107 Parente, *The Angels*, 40.

108 The historical record indicates that this incident occurred sometime around the year 180 B.C.

the Syrian governor that the Temple of Jerusalem is full of money. He does this because he is an enemy of the Jewish leader, Onias, and wishes to supplant him as High Priest. What the nefarious Simon neglects to mention is that the money in the Temple treasury is a fund for Hebrew widows and orphans, not a pile of cash to be spent at will.

The corrupt King of Asia, Seleucus, gets wind of this and promptly dispatches his henchman, Heliodorus, to "requisition" the money from the Jews. When Heliodorus arrives and informs the High Priest of his intentions, Onias and all Israel panic. Heliodorus says, "…this money must be confiscated for the royal treasury."

Like Hezekiah, Onias gathers the people in prayer and fasting during their moment of crisis. The Jewish leaders and people clearly understand that the aggressive act of a hostile government will profane their Temple, and the people's prayer saves the Temple from desecration (2 Macc 3:13b-15. 18).

Indeed, *at the very moment* they are united in prayer in the Temple, God sends three of His heavenly servants to teach Heliodorus a lesson about reverence. "Just as Heliodorus was arriving at the treasury with his bodyguards," it says,

> …there appeared to them a richly caparisoned horse, mounted by a fearsome rider. Charging furiously, the horse attacked Heliodorus with its front hooves. The rider was seen wearing golden armor. Then two other young men, remarkably strong, strikingly handsome, and splendidly attired, appeared before him. Standing on each side of him, they flogged him unceasingly, inflicting innumerable blows. Suddenly he fell to the ground, enveloped in great darkness. His men picked him up and laid him on a stretcher. (2 Macc 3:22-28)

Poor Heliodorus. He has to be among a select few in history who actually got beaten up by angels! Note that these "young men" were "remarkably strong, strikingly handsome, and splendidly attired". This is how angels look and dress when they take on human form. There are no homely angels.

Rarely do we see such drama from angels. They usually work behind the scenes, but this event was witnessed by everyone in the Temple that day because the passage says that "the people praised the Lord who had marvelously glorified his own place". The effect of the angels' actions was equally striking: "the temple, charged so shortly before with fear and commotion, was filled with joy and gladness, now that the almighty Lord had appeared" (2 Macc 3:30).

The angels' mission was not over. The High Priest Onias didn't want to be blamed for the actions of the heavenly security detail, so he offered an expiatory sacrifice for the unfortunate Heliodorus. The *same two angels* then came back to make sure that Heliodorus clearly understood the significance of the High Priest's prayer for him:

> While the high priest was offering the sacrifice of atonement, the same young men dressed in the same clothing again appeared and stood before Heliodorus. "Be very grateful to the high priest Onias," they told him. "It is for his sake that the Lord has spared your life. Since you have been scourged by Heaven, proclaim to all God's great power." When they had said this, they disappeared. (2 Macc 3:33-34)

After Heliodorus heals from his severe beating, he returns to his land to become a "witness to the deeds of the most high that he had seen with his own eyes" (36). The tumultuous incident ends on a humorous note.

When the Asian king later asked him who might be a suitable candidate to send back to Jerusalem to get the money, Heliodorus wryly responds: "If you have an enemy or one who is plotting against the government, send him there, and you will get him back with a flogging, if indeed he survives at all…" (38a).

Apparently, Heliodorus got the message.

10

ARTISTS, RESCUE OUR ANGELS!

Two wraith-like figures float in the air next to plumes of billowing white smoke framing a blackness that descends on the small town below them. Red flames pierce the darkened sky. The specters stand apart from the towering inferno, as if their very presence is an antidote to the burning corruption of the world.

Their garments, the color of ash, are little more than outlines on the canvas, indistinct and menacing in appearance. One of the figures holds up a thin, terrible sword that has just stuck its blow.

These beings are not of this world. Neither are they disturbed by the flames that have engulfed the town below their feet. Their only interest is in fulfilling God's will, as their haloes signify.

They are the angel punishers of Sodom and Gomorrah. He has sent them to cast fire upon the earth.

Such is the portrayal of holy angels by Gustave Moreau (1826-1898), a French Symbolist artist. His *Angels of Sodom* (ca. 1890) communicates in simple and remarkable imagery a number of truths about angelic beings: they are ethereal, powerful, holy, separated from all wickedness, ministers of God's immutable will, etc.[109]

---

[109] Please take a moment to do an Internet search for this image. I recall the very first time I set eyes on it. I said "Wow!" out loud. Even though Moreau was influenced by the Italian Renaissance in his biblical and classical works, he seems to have avoided the Renaissance's negative influence on angel images!

SPIRITUAL NATURES IN ART

In previous chapters I hinted at the difficulty of envisioning or representing angels in art. There is no truly adequate way to graphically depict an invisible being. Writers and artists can only do so with more or less fidelity to the truth about them. Depictions of angels that have *theological* accuracy – that is, that take into account the teaching about their spiritual natures – are the most adequate.

As I said before, humans are humans and angels are angels, but artists cannot avoid using human images to portray the persons of angels. The most skilled artists do so, however, in a way that accurately reflects the angels' fiery nature rather than reducing them to fluffy human beings with wings.

Some eras of art are more offensive than others in this regard, as Malcolm Godwin in his book *Angels: An Endangered Species,* observes:

> However beautiful, fascinating or real the images seem... the angelic fictions by artists of the Renaissance must be considered amongst the most fanciful flights of imagination ever conceived.[110]

As the quote expresses well, Renaissance (and, I would add, Baroque) art has had a net negative effect on how we understand angels. Most artists of these periods did a poor job of expressing angels' true spiritual nature.

Christian artists need to re-imagine the Renaissance versions of angels by putting angels back into proper theological perspective.

THE ROTTEN RENAISSANCE

The offending periods are the eras of European art history that span the 14th through 18th Centuries, roughly 1450-1600 for the Renaissance and 1600-1750 for the Baroque era. These periods are sandwiched between the Middle Ages (before) and the Enlightenment (after). To narrow the field of view a little further, our observations are limited

---

110 Malcolm Godwin, *Angels: An Endangered Species* (NY: Simon and Schuster, 1990), 169.

primarily to the art produced in the *Italian* Renaissance and Baroque periods.[111] I'm calling it all the Rotten Renaissance.

Modern culture's mental picture of angels is largely Renaissance Italian: Raphael's swan-winged, fair-haired children bent over lutes or mandolins; Botticelli's cleft-chinned, coiffed, princely angels staring blithely out at the viewer from the canvas; or the bored-looking, wide-eyed winged babies with elbows resting on a ledge in heaven waiting for something to happen.

These images are ubiquitous on Christmas cards and in religious art, which is a testimony to their durability. As evidence, I'll propose a simple test: what image comes to mind when you think of St. Michael the Archangel in art?

If you're like me, you probably call up the holy card picture of a fair-haired St. Michael wearing a skirt-like Roman Legion uniform, standing on top of an ugly, bat-like devil, thrusting a sword toward his head. Some depictions feature a lance; it doesn't matter. They are all variations on Guido Reni (ca. 1635), one of the greatest offenders of the Baroque era.[112]

I don't find Guido Reni's Michael, in *The Archangel Michael defeating Satan,* at all impressive, even with armor and sword. The angel's cocked head and limp stance is lackluster and unconvincing for the most powerful being in the heavenly host, and he stands over the devil rather *delicately* for a conquering hero.

To give proper credit, the Italian Renaissance and Baroque periods produced a massive amount of exquisite art, but angels were not their crowning achievement.

ANGELS OF COMFORT - NO!

Humans seem to have a psychological need to make angels into what *we want them to be* rather than what they really are: natures of fire and fierce warriors. Most Italian Renaissance angels are bland figures who might jump to your aid but probably wouldn't hurt a flea.

---

111 In the next chapter we will do a survey of artists of these and other periods who did not fall prey to the Rotten Renaissance angelology.

112 This painting can be found in the Church of Santa Maria della Concezione de Cappuccini in Rome.

The only example in the bible of an angel providing comfort is the incident of Jesus' suffering in the Garden of Gethsemane (Lk 22:43), but even there, the passage describes the angel as "strengthening" Jesus (reminiscent of Elijah's experience in the desert, 1 Kgs 17), not *comforting* Him in an emotional sense. The truth is that angels do not have emotions and therefore are totally devoid of human sentimentality.

Angels defend, strengthen, and encourage. They often exhort or refocus the person they are sent to assist, but they don't coddle or comfort. Angels are dispassionate executors of God's will. They radiate pure charity, not emotion. C.S. Lewis captured this characteristic perfectly in his novel *Perelandra*:

> The faces surprised him very much. Nothing less like the "angel" of popular art could well be imagined….One single changeless expression – so clear that it hurt and dazzled him – was stamped on each, and there was nothing else there at all….Here there was no affection at all….Pure, spiritual, intellectual love shot from their faces like barbed lightning. It was so unlike the love we experience that its expression could easily be mistaken for ferocity.[113]

Is it too much to ask for Christian artists to stop depicting angels as nice and pretty and fashionable and to start conveying the theological truth about them? Is it possible for artists to paint "ferocity"? There's the challenge.

FEROCITY WRAPPED IN INNOCENCE

Despite their powerful natures, angels are pure and innocent, which is why angels are often depicted as children.[114] There is nothing wrong with representing angels as children as long as the depictions reflect the theological truth of angelic power and beauty. It takes

---

113 I am greatly indebted to Peter Kreeft for highlighting this aspect of C.S. Lewis's angelology in his section on angelic love; cf. Kreeft, *Angels (and Demons)*, 88-90.

114 Throughout his whole life Padre Pio was gifted with actual sight of his guardian angel – who always appeared to the saint as a little boy. Depiction of angels as children is not a "fanciful flight of imagination", as is an effeminate portrayal.

a clear theological mind and a fine sense of perspective for an artist to get this paradox right.

French Baroque artist Georges de La Tour is unsurpassed in this respect. A brief analysis of one of La Tour's works, *The Dream of Joseph*[115] (1645), shows how La Tour effectively combined childlike innocence and angelic power in one powerful image.

His canvas shows a mature-looking child of seven or eight standing in front of an aged, sleeping St. Joseph. The angel is communicating a message to the foster father of Jesus in a dream as per the visions described in Matthew 1 and 2.

The child's face and gesturing hand are lit by the light of a single candle against the dark background, emphasizing the angel's role as a messenger of light. Though a child, the painting's perspective makes the angel look taller than the seated Joseph, as if to point out the superiority of the angelic nature. To depict a *child angel* giving a message about the Christ Child is breathtaking – and theologically astute. (Did I mention that La Tour was not Italian?)

TIME TO PURGE INACCURACIES

In short, it's time to retire the hackneyed, inaccurate Italian Renaissance angels and replace them with truly striking images of angels that are faithful to the truth of their spiritual natures. First let's clear away four *categories* of angels that ought to be purged from the Christian artist's repertoire:

1. Child angels, yes; baby angels, no

There are no baby angels in scripture, and pre-Renaissance Christian artists never depicted angels as babies. Donatello seems to have begun the trend in the 1400s, and other artists, unfortunately, picked up on it.

Chubby, naked babies with wings plucking lyres are not angels at all. They received the name *putto* ("child" or "boy", pl. *putti*) during the Renaissance period because they resembled similar figures carved onto the sides of ancient sarcophagi, particularly the tombs of children.

---

115 This image can be easily discovered through an Internet search.

But these figures were symbols of the Roman god Cupid (Greek, Eros), who was often represented as a little boy.[116]

The transposition of the *putti* into Christian art had the effect of confusing the pagan god of erotic love with angels. How that happened is anyone's guess, but it was one of the more unfortunate developments of religious art.

Then, in some bizarre twist of historical fate, artists began to call these figures "cherubs", as if the actual Cherubim of scripture were tiny, baby-like, non-threatening creatures who made people feel good. The name is totally misplaced. The image of a harp-playing baby with puppy-dog eyes is a mockery of the fierce Cherubim revealed in the pages of scripture. Read the first chapter of the Book of Ezekiel if you doubt me on this point.

Modern artists should entirely eliminate the concept of *putto* or baby cherub from their repertoire when portraying angels in religious art. They are pure fiction and bad art.

2. Male or female angels, yes; androgynous angels, no

Artists need to start depicting powerful, warlike angels that are true to their biblical precedents. As I mentioned in Chapter 4, angels are exclusively males in scripture, but artistic license undoubtedly permits artists to portray angels as females as long as they express the truth of the angelic nature and mission.

European art is full of strong, virtuous, even warlike, such as ancient goddesses or the biblical Judith decapitating the Assyrian general Holofernes (Jdt 13:1-10). The exploits of Deborah, the prophet and judge of Israel (Jdg 4 and 5), were another favorite of Christian artists. So a feminine angel could communicate force, virtue, strength, and the adamant service of God just as easily as a masculine angel.

Artists should not, however, depict as female those angels whom scripture has revealed in masculine terms. The specific content of God's revelation binds the Christian artist as well as the theologian. In other words, no Saint *Gabriella* the Archangel, please.[117]

---

116 In the myth of Cupid and Psyche he is represented as a young man.
117 The Hebrew name, Gabriel actually means "warrior" or "strongman" of God.

Male or female angels are fine, but angels that express neither masculine virtue nor feminine heroism should be anathema to Christian art.

3. Angels in skirts – absolutely no!

As noted numerous times in this book, angels leave men literally awe-struck whenever they appear, which means that dreary angel art does them a great injustice. Artists in the past five centuries have repeated the patterns of the Rotten Renaissance by presenting angels as cherubic babies, supernatural fashion mavens, or as adolescent girls playing violins for the Holy Family on the flight into Egypt.

Angels also suffer from another type of deformation. The Renaissance initiated a trend of presenting God's warriors as androgynous youths in effeminate poses or wearing skirts (à la Guido Reni). Feminized features superimposed on male bodies are a grotesque misrepresentation of angelic virtue and power. If angels of that type actually existed, the devil would have nothing to fear from them.

There is a weak attempt at theology behind these depictions. Angels are spiritual beings, so, technically speaking, they are genderless, as noted in Chapter 4. There again, the theology is skewed: genderless does not mean androgynous!

Prior to the Renaissance, particularly in eastern iconography, artists pictured St. Michael and his warrior angels in majestic garb or in the war gear of their day. (Medieval depictions often show angels in the full body armor of the warrior knight.) Byzantine iconographers usually showed angels in robes, but these were culturally accurate and not feminized garments such as women's dresses or skirts.

Italian Renaissance artists, however, generally portrayed St. Michael and other angels as androgynous-looking Roman soldiers with short skirt, open chest, flowing cape, and decorative leggings, or variations on that theme. They broke from tradition and began a toxic trend of androgyny which skewed our theological understanding of true angelic power and glory.

Every now and then we come across a skilled painter or sculptor who depicts the skirt-like Roman uniform in a way that is complementary to a strongly masculine appearance, but these are rare. There are very few cases in which the "skirt" is not a distraction to the communication of a religious message.

To emphasize the point, St. Joan of Arc made an exasperated comment when she was asked by an interrogator whether St. Michael the Archangel, who appeared to her, had any clothes on. "My goodness," she cried, "do you think God cannot clothe His angels?" Good point. The only thing lacking in depicting angelic garb is the human imagination.

Modern artists: no skirts on angels!

4. Cartoonish angels - please, no!

Fast-forward half a millennium to the modern graphic trend of depicting angels as ninja warriors, occult fighters, or Rambo-like body builders. This is the inverse of the feminizing trend noted in the last two points but is equally toxic.

Many younger artists attempt to create cool warrior angels for video games. But all video game angels I've seen are cartoonish, by definition of the medium itself. Given the immature audience, that is understandable but not acceptable. Macho video angels sometimes wear up-to-date Kevlar armor and carry elaborate swords or other bizarre weapons which attempt to add effect to their virtual killing sprees. These are angels for the "spiritual but not religious" types who pay more attention to social media trends than they do to matters of faith.

Apart from these adolescent distortions, the cultural problem is actually much deeper: it is often impossible to distinguish angels from demons in occult-themed graphics. This existential ambiguity in modern art mirrors the androgyny of the Renaissance and Baroque periods.

Art that cannot define gender differences or the clear lines between good and evil creates spiritual confusion that can only be detrimental to the souls of young people. It distorts the truth about angels.

MISSION FIELDS RIPE FOR THE HARVEST

Christian artists have a duty to put angels back into their proper context of faith and theological truth. Evangelization through beauty is the Christian artist's mandate.[118] Not only that, but we live in the midst of a generation saturated with unclean images and strong currents of angel-worshipping occultism, so the mission fields are ripe for a harvest of excellent angel art.

Here are a few fields of modern culture that, with a little artistic imagination, could benefit from an infusion of angelic beauty, truth, and goodness:

1. The realm of science and technology

Were angels present at the Big Bang? A clever artist could answer that. Since angels are given charge over the elements of the universe, they *must have* been there. But what would that have looked like?

How about angelic involvement in the earth-shattering discoveries of modern physics, molecular biology, quantum mechanics, bioethics, and medicine? Surely human beings aren't the only ones who know anything about these sciences. Imagine an angel standing nobly by an equation-filled chalkboard whispering theories into a genius's ear.

A talented artist could paint holy angels as patrons and protectors of the stars, the universe, the earth, planets and their satellites, planetary movements and conjunctions, eclipses, galaxies, black holes, red dwarfs, nebulae, pulsars, and other cosmic phenomena. With scientifically accurate and imaginative art, the Church would have a better chance of fighting the New Age and witchcraft movements that use these forces for their own deceptive purposes.

2. The realm of history and politics

Scripture frequently presents angels as influencing the course of

---

118 Jem Sullivan, PhD, *The Beauty of Faith: Using Christian Art to Spread the Good News* (Huntington: Our Sunday Visitor, Inc., 2009), 89. In this marvelous book, Sullivan speaks of the challenges of a "culture of images" for evangelization but gives very practical recommendations for evangelizing through art. *The Beauty of Faith* is a must-read for serious Christian artists and all who are devoted to beauty; Pope John Paul II, *Letter to Artists*, 1999, 3.

history and playing roles in actual historical events.[119] Have angels stopped doing that in the modern age?

Angels have made their mark on human events for good and for ill (demons). An artist could illustrate the role of demons in the horrible wars of the 20th century or the mass murders by godless ideologues or terrorists. Why not show the holy angels *containing* the evils or rescuing people from evil, as in the famous incident of the Angels of Mons in the First World War? Many witnesses of that battle told of the intervention of numerous ethereal beings whose presence seemed to shift the tide of the Battle of Mons (November 1915) to the Allies at a decisive moment.

Our generation needs to see angels with soldiers on battlefields, angels accompanying martyrs in their prisons and to their deaths, perhaps even angels meting out justice to the liars and wicked leaders who have essentially deconstructed Western civilization in the past few centuries.[120]

3. The realm of the Church and her mission

Angels promote and amplify the Church's mission in all ages, which is why the Acts of the Apostles shows so many angels helping the first Christians spread the gospel everywhere. Have they stopped helping the Church? Artists could easily find new ways to picture this very angelic role:

- Angel custodians of the seven Sacraments;

- Angels as bridges between the Church Militant, the Church Suffering, and the Church Triumphant;

---

119 A few biblical examples: saving people from slavery and oppression (Egypt, Ex 3-15); executing judgment (Sodom, Gen 19); preventing evil and destruction (Assyria, 2 Kgs 19); opening new avenues for the gospel (to Samaria, Acts 8; to Macedonia, Acts 16); protecting all things holy (the People of Israel, Ex 23; the Temple, 2 Macc 5; the Apostles, Acts 8); even striking down evil rulers (Herod, Acts 12).

120 For example, in his book *Modern Times*, historian Paul Johnson recounted the story of the death of the notorious mass murderer Joseph Stalin. The event has every mark of demons coming to claim one of their own at the moment Stalin died. Cf. Paul Johnson, *Modern Times: From the Twenties to the Nineties* (New York: Harper Collins Publishers, 1993), 456.

- Angels assisting exorcists in delivering people from demonic oppression;
- Angels of music, preaching, and sacred liturgy;
- Angels motivating and assisting the missionary work of the Church;
- Angels involved in dramatic conversions; and so many more!

We also need artists to keep pious souls from falling into a sort of sappy devotionalism that is as dangerous to authentic faith as secularism. It would be a great service to the Church if artists would re-imagine certain angel appearances associated with Marian apparitions and other mystical visions.

It is almost impossible, for example, to find a truly striking rendering of the Angel of Fatima.[121] The main visionary of Fatima, Sister Lucía, described the same angel in words that beg for artistic expression:

> [A]t the left of Our Lady and a little above, we saw an Angel with a flaming sword in his left hand; flashing, it gave out flames that looked as though they would set the world on fire; but they died out in contact with the splendour that Our Lady radiated towards him from her right hand: pointing to the earth with his right hand, the Angel cried out in a loud voice: "Penance, Penance, Penance!"[122]

The same can be said for the well-known mystical experiences of saints and their guardian angels. The story of St. Francis and the Seraph who imprinted the stigmata on him, for example, needs serious updating from the 14th century painting by Giotto and its many hackneyed copies. The stories of St. John Bosco's guardian angel, who often came

---

[121] This angel identified himself as the Angel of Portugal and appeared three times to the shepherd children prior to the 1917 apparitions of the Virgin Mary in Fatima, Portugal.

[122] On May 13th, 2000 the Vatican's Congregation for the Doctrine of the Faith revealed the alleged Third Secret of Fatima with an interpretative commentary. The above text was part of Sr. Lucia's description of her mystical experience.

dressed as a *grey dog*, need new artistic life. St. Faustina, St. Angela of Foligno, St. Gemma Galgani and Padre Pio all had direct experiences of their angels.

Clearly, the possibilities are endless for depicting the work of the holy angels in every dimension of the Church's life and mission. Christian artists should be *rushing* to depict such scenes.

MORE GLORY, NOT LESS

The artists of the Italian Renaissance and Baroque periods helped save Catholicism from the ravages of the Reformation, but I believe they did a great disservice to the artistic imagination in the process, at least as regards angels. They gave a largely sentimentalized view of angels to generations of future artists.

Portraying angels as comfortable friends, pudgy babies, effeminate adolescents, or hapless companions on our journeys is easy, but it's wrong. Angels are much more majestic and wonderful than these images portray.

The next and final chapter of this book is a brief commentary on some of history's best angel artists. Any angel aficionado will benefit from doing internet searches for the angels on the list. Wouldn't it be inspirational to see modern artists pick up the torch of the great angel artists of the past and carry the fire into the 21st century?

Christian artists, we need you to rescue our angels. We need *more* glory now, not less.

11

ACCURATE ANGEL ART

The reason I love St. Joan of Arc so much is not only that she was angelic and fierce but also that she met St. Michael the Archangel *personally*. Imagine that encounter! The 19th century French artist, Eugene Thirion (1839-1910) did just that. He captured that singular moment perfectly in his remarkable 1876 work, entitled simply *Jeanne d'Arc*.

Joan, dressed in the tones of earth (dark green, red, and brown), is sitting upright on a rock in the center of the canvas. She is holding a spindle of flax, which she drops at the moment she's overcome by the arrival of the heavenly visitor. According to the historical account, the Maid saw the angel with her own eyes, but in Thirion's image she only hears him whisper in her ear as he descends from on high and floats on a cloud *behind* her – parallel to but not touching the earth.

Michael holds a sword in one hand and with the other points into a patch of radiant cloud, perhaps in the direction of a distant battlefield. He is handsome, a male in the prime of youth dressed in a sky blue robe that loosely envelops him as he floats near the saint. He is her voice from heaven who speaks a divine word, a message to which we are not privy, but Joan's wide eyes indicate that she is transfixed by its power.

She gazes outward from the canvas into an invisible world. We imagine she is envisioning the terms of the mission God is asking of her. Is her look one of fear, awe, contemplation, wonder, shock? The viewer must decide. That look is certainly *not* the glassy-eyed stare of a daydreamer.

Above and beyond Michael, framed by his white wings, another angel dressed in armor blows a horn that summons men to combat. This heavenly sentinel looks away from Joan to where Michael is pointing and holds a banner remarkably similar to the one Joan would carry into battle years later.

The scene is gripping, the colors remarkable, every detail crisp and inspired. The two faces, the girl's and the angel's, seem to emerge from the center of the canvas into the viewer's space. The vivid snapshot on canvas makes one feel he is actually standing in front of the Maid at her first shocking encounter with the great Archangel. It is accurate angel art.

In the last chapter I tried to make the case that good angel art reflects a proper theological understanding of their nature and mission and draws us into a contemplation of spiritual realities, as Thirion's work does. Bad angel art exudes sentimentality. But that still leaves us with the question: If angels are invisible, what *are* they supposed to look like on a canvas?

Thankfully, we don't have to guess at an answer. Art history (but not the Italian Renaissance!) abounds with images that accurately portray the truth about angels, and we have to look for them. In the following pages we will examine a few of the best angel images and artists worth studying.

1. THE PRE-RENAISSANCE PERIOD

The Book of Kells (Irish, c. 800) – The *Book of Kells* is a marvelous illuminated manuscript of the Latin bible produced by monks from the Emerald Isle in the 9th century. One bright panel from this bible (Folio 27, the Gospel of Matthew) shows the four evangelists depicted in the form of Ezekiel's Cherubim. It's sublime in its beauty, not to mention its biblical accuracy.

Giotto (Italian, 1266-1337) – The greatest of the masters of the pre-Renaissance period helped to bring art out of its Byzantine formalism.

Giotto's angels are more iconographic than those of later artists, but they have a spiritual depth that exudes truth and great beauty. Giotto accurately depicts the love and holiness of these spiritual beings. The pathos of the heavenly angels weeping over the death of Christ in Giotto's *Lamentation* is something to behold.

The Apocalypse Tapestries of Angers (French, late 1300s) – These seventy-eight medieval masterpieces are not oil paintings but vast weavings of various scenes in the Book of Revelation, many of which contain angels. They are exquisite works created to adorn the palace walls of John I, Duke of Anjou (brother of the French King Charles V) in the period following the dreaded Black Death of the 14th century.[123] It is hard to imagine the artistry involved in such detailed works being created in the medium of wool cloth rather than paint or sculpture.

The Trinity Icon (Russian, c. 1425) – This icon was written[124] by the famous Andrei Rublev and is considered the "mother of all icons" due to its timeless beauty and spiritual depth. It depicts the scene in Genesis 18 in which three angels visit Abraham and Sarah to announce the birth of Isaac. The angels are an allegory of the three Persons of the Most Holy Trinity; there are no angels in the history of human art so worthy of contemplation as those of Rublev.

2. NORTHERN EUROPEAN RENAISSANCE

Teutonic angels, as I call them, better depict the spiritual nature and mission of the angels than those of the Italian Renaissance. They are more like C.S. Lewis's fiercely charitable angels in *Perelandra*, as mentioned in the last chapter. Northern European artists often picture

---

123 Historian Barbara Tuchman's commentary on the Duke of Anjou's lavish expense for these tapestries is insightful: "In the second half of the 14th century [ostentation and pageantry] went to extremes, as if to defy the increased uncertainty of life. Conspicuous consumption became a frenzied excess, a gilded shroud over the Black Death and lost battles, a desperate desire to show oneself fortunate in a time of advancing misfortune." Barbara W. Tuchman, *A Distant Mirror: The Calamitous 14th Century* (New York: Random House, 1978), 256.

124 Icons are considered "words" from God and the inspired artist is seen as the "revealer" of the word rather than an individual self-expressive artist in his own right. Hence, it is proper to speak of the creation of an icon as the artist "writing" rather than "painting" it.

warrior angels in the middle of ferocious battles, or servile angels in very attentive poses, assisting their charges with unsentimental gazes and detached charity. The exception to this rule is the Baroque period of Germanic art (1600-1750) which was highly influenced by Italian-style "putti".

Jan Van Eyck (early Netherlandish/Flemish, 1395-1441) – Van Eyck's masterpiece called *The Adoration of the Mystic Lamb* is a portion of the twelve-panel Ghent Altarpiece created in 1432. This work of genius "ranks among the most significant works of art in Europe".[125] The center of the scene is the Lamb of God standing on an altar with adoring angels all around. The angels have multi-colored wings and some of them are swinging censers full of incense! Certainly Van Eyck's angels are excellent examples of glorious Teutonic angels doing what angels do best: adoring God.

Hans Memling (early Netherlandish/Flemish, 1430-1496) – Memling's *Last Judgment* (1471) features St. Michael the Archangel dressed in full battle armor at the center of the painting. He is weighing souls on a large scale while other Teutonic angels, holding various elements of the Passion, attend to Jesus the Righteous Judge in the panel above. The angels in Memling's *Annunciation* are of such beauty and incredible delicacy that they are hard to describe in words.

Martin Schöngauer (German Renaissance, 1440–1491) – Schöngauer stands in the tradition of the finest German engravers. His woodcut of *St. Michael* fighting the devil (1477) is simply extraordinary! Not only is St. Michael inspiring as a holy warrior, but the multi-tentacled Lucifer is intense, riveting, even frightening – as demons should be depicted in art.

Albrecht Dürer (German Renaissance, 1471-1528) – Dürer is most noted for his engraving of the *Praying Hands,* as well as his fifteen

---

125 That is the assessment of the restorers of this masterpiece. Jan worked with his brother Hubert, who was the illustrator. You can see the whole magnificent restoration at an interactive digital website, "Closer to Van Eyck: Rediscovering the Ghent Altarpiece" at *http://closertovaneyck.kikirpa.be.*

woodcuts in the amazing *Apocalypse* series (1498). The cuts are masterpieces of Teutonic angels in action, particularly the most celebrated print in the series, the "Four Horsemen". Among the many other angels in the series are the "Angels Holding Back the Four Winds", "The Angel with the Key to the Abyss", and "The Four Angels of Death".

Peter Breugel (Dutch Renaissance, 1525-1569) – Breugel's *Fall of the Rebel Angels* shocks and inspires at the same time. The angels are full of fight, diving and weaving about a canvas full of demons and hacking away at them with swords. His depiction of angels stands in marked contrast to a work by a later contemporary, Peter Paul Rubens (Belgian Baroque), who depicts the apostate angels as stylish male nudes falling headlong out of the sky – ugh! (Rubens was highly influenced by the Italian Renaissance. Say no more.)

3. THE MODERN PERIOD

William Blake (English Romantic poet and artist, 1757-1827) – Blake was some sort of visionary who left accounts of his mystical experiences in poetry and art. He was also a voluminous angel artist, though not all of his renderings are attractive (some in fact are a bit cartoonish). Many of them, however, are quite striking, such as the *Angel Rolling Away the Resurrection Stone*. He also painted a series of twelve scenes from the Book of Revelation, of which the four incredible "Great Red Dragon" paintings are essential material for any serious student of religious art.

William Turner (English, 1789-1862) – Turner was a Romantic artist primarily known for his incredible land and seascapes; however, his one angel depiction, *The Angel, Standing in the Sun*, is a truly fascinating work depicting in brilliant light and color one of the glorious angels of the Apocalypse.

John Martin (English Romantic, 1789-1854) – Martin created a series of forty-eight mezzotints (burnished images on metal plates) between 1824 and 1827 in which he depicted all the major scenes of Milton's epic poem *Paradise Lost*. In the words of one commentator: "Martin's work was completely original…. his visions of Heaven and Hell, of the conflict between Good and Evil, between the Heavenly Host and Satan are spectacularly original in their drama and scope, a summit of Romantic art".[126]

Gustave Moreau (French Symbolist, 1826-1898) – Moreau's *Angels of Sodom* (which I described at the beginning of Chapter 10) must surely stand as one of the most breathtaking images of angels ever painted. The two representatives of God who hover over the city of Sodom inspire a profound horror of the terrible consequences of sin.

Arnold Böcklin (Swiss Symbolist, 1827-1901) – Böcklin was not an angel artist per se, but his depiction of the destroying angel of Egypt in *The Plague* (1898) is heart-stopping.

Gustave Doré (French, 1832-1883) – This famous French illustrator created many series of engravings for publication, including Milton's *Paradise Lost* (following John Martin) and 136 plates for Dante's *Divine Comedy*. His depictions of the latter's *Paradiso* show myriads of extremely elegant angels in "The Heaven of the Fixed Stars", "Circle of Angels", and "Angels in Heaven". The scene for "Lucifer the King of Hell" for his *Inferno* series can only be described as harrowing.

James Tissot (French Realist, 1836-1902) – Tissot created his best artwork after the 1885 revival of his Catholic faith. During the rest of his productive life, he illustrated most of the scenes of the Old Testament and painted a series entitled *The Life of Our Savior Jesus Christ* in a style that is striking for its portrayal of a diverse array of Middle Eastern figures. Tissot's "Annunciation", "Temptations of Jesus", and "Soul of the Penitent Thief in Paradise" (who is transported by angels with burning censers) are all spectacular and have to be seen to be believed. These are just a few of the extremely perceptive paintings of angels in Tissot's spectacular oeuvre.

---

126 John Martin's *Paradise Lost* mezzotints (1824-1827) from the 1827 Prowett Edition, 3/20/12, http://www.spaightwoodgalleries.com/Pages/Martin.html, accessed on 8/8/20.

Edward Burne-Jones (British Pre-Raphaelite/Symbolist, 1833-1898) – Burne-Jones was a prodigy of the arts and crafts movement in 19th century England, working fluidly and masterfully in ceramic, jewelry, tapestries, mosaics, stained glass, church design, illustrating, and all modes of painting. His angels are perhaps the sweetest, loveliest creations of this long list of remarkable angel artists. One has only to lay eyes on the angels in his watercolor *Days of Creation* (1876) or contemplate the majestic angel who holds *The Star of Bethlehem* (1890) to understand that Burne-Jones has captured something more than just a spark of the innocence and beauty of God's holy ones.

4. CONTEMPORARY ARTISTS

This brief survey ends with four stained glass artists of the past century. Holy angels can be beautifully depicted using light as an art form because they were present with God when "the true light, which enlightens everyone" (Jn 1:9) came into the world.

Marc Chagall (Russian-French Surrealist, 1887-1985) – Chagall's paintings and stained glass works are considered "gardens of color", replete with angels from virtually every Old Testament passage that portrays them. The angels in the five enormous stained glass windows (32 x 3 feet) he created for Fraumünster Church in Zurich, Switzerland in 1970 are unparalleled in their riotous color schemes, particularly the window depicting Jacob wrestling with an angel. In fact, angels populate Chagall's works more than any other contemporary artist.

Harry Clarke (Irish, stained glass, 1889-1931) – In my opinion, Clarke is the world's pre-eminent stained glass artist. His career was cut short by his untimely death of tuberculosis at the age of 41. Yet, in his relatively few productive years, Clarke left a legacy of the most exquisite glass the world has ever seen. Angels are only part of his stained glass work, of course, but his creativity in depicting angels was enchanting: he dressed them in the most delicate robes and colors, he gave them flight and intense piety, he made them look both innocent and fierce, and he even depicted angels so burning brightly with love for God that their hair was aflame!

Two Americans, **John La Farge** (1835-1910) and **Louis Comfort Tiffany** (1848-1933) were stained glass makers at the end of the nineteenth and early twentieth centuries. Through their creations, they enriched dozens of churches and brought beautiful angels into the secular culture. Their angels are not quite as refined as Clarke's or as rich in color as Chagall's, but they are beautiful and offer inspiring examples of angelic simplicity, nobility, and innocence. Both artists used a technique of opalescent glassmaking that allowed their windows to refract light in a way never seen before in the history of stained glass.

Tiffany was a canvas artist also. I am particularly enamored of his series of twelve angels (watercolors) entitled *Angels Representing Adoration, Praise, Thanksgiving, and Love*. There is also a *Pair of Tiffany Angel Windows* in a private collection that, in classic American style, is currently being sold on eBay for $175,000 – they are magnificent!

The wonders of modern technology make every one of the images named in these pages easily accessible to anyone with a computer and an Internet connection. Many others are accessible through libraries and museums. I invite all readers to drink deeply of the beauty and truth of the angels expressed in these masterpieces. Their type of accurate angel art is the only type we should endorse. They uplift heart and soul.

As sublime and worthy of contemplation as these works of art are, however, they are faint sparks of the glory of the otherworldly realities they represent. And if the holy angels are so wondrous, how much more their Maker?

Conclusion

PRAYING TO ANGELS

I would like to add one final testimony before we conclude: mine. All the teaching and artwork about angels pales in comparison to a highly personal experience of them. Angels are very real to me.

It happened one morning, nearly two decades ago, as I was driving on a wet highway to attend a prayer service. A gust of wind hit the back of my little Toyota truck and sent it into a tail spin. In an instant I found myself spiraling out of control in the middle of sixty-mile-an-hour traffic.

I don't know how it happened, but the little truck careened like a wobbly child's top through a gap in traffic on the congested highway without hitting a single car. I sat frozen in terror as the out-of-control truck headed toward the grassy median strip. I envisioned it plowing through the grass into oncoming traffic. I was as good as dead.

Then for some reason, I cried out, "Angel! Help!"

Flash. The spinning motion suddenly stopped, and the truck hit the median strip broadside. According to the laws of physics, the light truck should have flipped like one of those Indy 500 crashes – side over side, end over end, bolting up into the air before crashing down on top of the other cars in a fiery wipeout – but that didn't happen.

Call it a miracle, but as soon as the truck hit the grass, there appeared, as sure as I live, a *presence* outside my driver's window.

What I perceived in that instant "felt" like the presence of a very strong man who immediately gripped the top of my truck, handling it as easily as if he were lifting a light barbell in a gym.

Instantly, the truck's momentum ceased. I mean, the whole truck *stopped moving* – from sixty miles an hour to zero in a split second. It just stopped.

The truck then trundled calmly onto its side, and I saw the grass rise gently to my window as the cab was lowered to the ground. It was like one of those slow-motion movie clips that survivors sometimes perceive in the midst of a traumatic incident. I watched the side-view mirror push itself firmly into the sod, and then I blacked out.

A few Good Samaritans came to my rescue some minutes later, and soon I was in an ambulance rushing to the hospital, from which I was discharged shortly after with little more than a bump on my forehead. I survived what should have been a fatal crash.

Who was that strong man? Where did he come from so suddenly in my moment of need? Was it just a coincidence that the truck slid sideways through a mysterious gap in traffic? How did a spinning vehicle with such momentum stop on a dime like that? Why no serious injuries?

In light of the chapters you've just read, you should be able to answer all those questions as well as I.

THE SPIRITUAL QUESTION

A larger question remains, though. It is the spiritual question. As I said at the beginning, it's not the angel's primary job to keep us from drowning, but sometimes an angel does intervene to save a life. Yet, since auto accidents are one of the leading causes of death every year, they obviously *don't* intervene in millions of car crashes. Why was *I* saved from death?

Here again we find ourselves face-to-face with an analogy for understanding something critical about angels. Angel rescues teach a spiritual lesson, and my story is as good as anyone else's to communicate a sobering truth:

Saving us from bodily death signifies the guardian angels' primary mission of saving us from *a much worse death:* "And do not be afraid of those who kill the body but cannot kill the soul; rather, be afraid of the one who can destroy both soul and body in Gehenna" (Mt 10:28).

The loss of our immortal soul is the one thing we should fear. And we don't fear it nearly enough. Thankfully the angels do. They understand that Gehenna is eternal fire.

God fights fire with fire, remember?

Only in heaven will we see how diligently these natures of fire have watched over our souls on this earthly journey. Then, the full reason why God created angels will become crystal clear, and it will not be possible to thank them enough for their unselfish ministry to us.

PRAYER TO OUR ANGELS

So, can we pray to our guardian angels? Yes! We can and we should.

Prayer is an angel's native tongue. It is the most basic form of communication between spiritual beings; so, as (partly) spiritual beings ourselves, prayer is our high speed Internet connection to the angels. In the context of Christian prayer, contact with holy angels is safe and wholesome.

We should prioritize three types of prayer *to and with* the angels.

1. The Guardian Angel Prayer

Make a habit to pray this prayer every day. Learn it, teach it, and spread it as a form of personal devotion to the guardian angels. It is an ancient prayer of the Church that dates back nearly a thousand years![127]

The essence of this prayer is a personal address to the spiritual being Jesus Christ has given you to assist you on your way to heaven. You can feel entirely free to enter into spiritual conversation with your angel through prayer, respecting the limits we spoke of in Chapters 2 and 3.

As should be clear from Chapters 4 and 5, this will not be – cannot be – a normal human-to-human conversation. It will be more like a spirit-to-spirit dialogue about everything that concerns you,

---

[127] Historians trace the origin of the Latin prayer *Angele Dei* to Brother Reginald, a companion of St. Anselm in the 11th century. The English translation comes from the 19th century and has a wide acceptance throughout the English-speaking world.

particularly in matters of the spiritual life and the salvation of souls. Your guardian angel will teach you, through the circumstances of your life, to understand these concerns in the light of God's will.

And yes, of course, we can ask our guardian angels to assist our loved ones too. If we are concerned about people and their salvation, our angels are also concerned about them. Padre Pio used to "send" his guardian angel to the guardian angels of other people so the angels would work together for the good of the other.

This is not magic, and we should never expect quick-fix solutions to human problems from the angels. It's an act of faith. We believe the angels are involved in the lives of human beings and that they're more concerned about human souls than most people are for their own souls. The angels honor and assist every honest intention for the wellbeing of others, but always remember that your guardian angel's primary mission is the welfare of *your* soul.

2. The Prayer for Opening

All of the angelic ministries detailed in Chapter 1 are vital angelic works, but I personally believe that our guardian angels delight most of all in opening pathways of grace to us in this world. If the deadliest work of the devil is to enslave us in sin, the most potent work of the good angels is to liberate us from his grip.

That means they can turn on lights to scatter the darkness, unchain us from our prisons, and blast open spiritual floodgates to let the purifying graces of heaven flood our souls. The guardian angels are experts at opening things.

We all have our own private frustrations, blockages, and sinful habits to deal with, and the angels are more aware of these threats than we are. Ask your guardian angel for help in personal conversion and in fulfilling the duties of your state in life. Guardian angels love to free us from the constraints of the world, the flesh, and the devil – but we must ask for their help.

3. Prayers of Adoration

The New Age movement makes the mistake of thinking that angels are at our beck and call whenever we need their services. That's because a non-Christian view of angels overlooks their first and primary function: adoration. Angels do not come at our beck and call. They come at God's.

The prayers our guardian angels honor most are prayers of adoration. These are not prayers *to* the angels, as in numbers 1 and 2 above. They are prayers *with* the angels. Whenever we enter into the act of adoration, our angels augment and bless such prayers. They teach us how and why to adore God. They instill reverence and purity of heart in our worship.

Take your angel with you to Mass and invite your angel's help any time you enter into prayer and worship. The Book of Revelation shows thousands of angels participating in the eternal adoration of the Lamb; their liturgy in heaven is an extension of our liturgical prayer on earth (or perhaps ours is an extension of theirs).

They offer our prayers to God on a fiery altar in heaven like the incense we offer on altars here below:

> Another angel came and stood at the altar, holding a gold censer. He was given a great quantity of incense to offer, along with the prayers of all the holy ones, on the gold altar that was before the throne. The smoke of the incense along with the prayers of the holy ones went up before God from the hand of the angel. (Rev 8:3-4)

So let us never hesitate to offer generous prayers to and with our guardian angels. And let us trust in their unwavering love for us and their desire to see us join them one day in the Kingdom of blessedness, where every tear of this sad world will be wiped away (Rev 21:4).

Then, together with them, we will adore the Lord eternally and bask forever in that river of spiritual fire that issues from His Throne.

Appendix 1

FIRE AND ICE

If God's angels are fire, then Satan's angels – demons – are ice, in a spiritual sense. And needless to say, fire and ice don't mix.

I'm speaking here not of a difference in their natures, which are both angelic, but in the character of their personalities. Angels and demons are spiritual persons in every sense, endowed with intellect and will, created with a personal ego and identity, which is to say that both angels and demons have a very personal involvement in their respective missions. They put their whole personalities into their objectives, for good or evil.

ICE-COLD PERSONALITIES

Scripture and the Church's teaching on hell suggest that the state of damnation is a kind of torture of flames (which I hope I never have to verify by personal experience), but that's not a description of the demonic personality. Demons have nothing of warmth in them in any sense – they are ice angels.

We understand physical cold as an absence of warmth. Spiritual cold (evil), then, is an absence of goodness, just like darkness is an absence of light. Demons *as persons* lack any shred of goodness or light.

The fallen angels were created good but chose to reject God's plan of salvation, which involved exalting human nature over the angels through Christ. Some of them chose not to serve God and lost their place in heaven. At the same moment, they lost their original innocence, the state of grace and every virtue, although they retained the natural powers of intellect and will that God gave them.

Like a black hole – a patch of outer space turned in on itself – the fallen angels' rebellion drained them of all truth, beauty, and goodness, which are essential attributes of God's personality, if we may call it that. At their fall, the demons were entirely corrupted, turned inside out. They became the essence of lies, ugliness, and evil. That's what happens when you reject God.

In his famous work *The Inferno*, the medieval poet Dante Alleghieri had an intuition of this inversion of the right order of things when he placed Lucifer at the lowest point of hell encased in ice, chewing for all eternity on Judas, the traitor, and Brutus, the betrayer of Julius Caesar. For Dante, betrayal was the greatest sin because he considered it Satan's original sin against God.

Common sense also recognizes the difference between a person with a warm personality, full of goodness and life, versus someone with a frigid personality whose negative characteristics flow out of a life of misery or evil.

My sister tells the shocking story of a chance encounter she had with one of the 9/11 hijackers, Mohammed Ata, who came into a convenience store she was managing prior to the 2001 attack. She recalls a literal chill ran down her spine the moment she laid eyes on him. She didn't understand the ice-cold feeling at the time, but later she saw his picture identifying him as one of the hijackers, and then she understood the freezing aura the man's *very persona* seemed to exude.

In an even more penetrating way (because they are spiritual beings), demons are ice-cold spiritual vacuums, totally devoid of all good. They are malevolent personalities who have deliberately chosen their own personal hell away from God and against God. In so doing, their angelic mission became more sinister than the worst possible criminality we can imagine on earth. They know they cannot destroy God, so they propose to destroy *His children*.

In God's plan, however, they can only do that with our permission.

FEAR AND CONSENT

The Church's teaching is very clear about the power demons exercise over the world and can *potentially* exercise over human beings:

> According to Sacred Scripture…the dominion and the influence of Satan and of the other evil spirits embraces *all the world*. We may think of Christ's parable about the field (Mt 13:38-39), about the good seed and the bad seed that the devil sows in the midst of the wheat, seeking to snatch away from hearts the good that has been 'sown' in them (John Paul II, General Audience, August 13, 1986).

Because of their higher nature and natural gifts, they can harm us, but only if we are foolish enough to give them an opening. St. Padre Pio used to say that the devil is like a rabid dog on a chain. He can only do us harm if we come within the radius of his chain.

The Church is equally clear, however, about the superiority of the holy angels over the demons, and is unequivocal in the assertion that each of us has a personal guardian angel who protects us from them. In Chapter 6, I pointed out the teaching of Thomas Aquinas in this regard. Several images of the New Testament also affirm the restraining power of God's grace on the demons (see especially 2 Thes 2:7 and Rev 20:6).

The position of the believer towards demons then, must always be the balanced attitude of the Church. On the one hand, because they are superior beings we must *prudently fear* demons. On the other hand, because they are subordinate to the power of God and His holy angels, we should not *be afraid* of them in a sense of unwarranted paranoia that they are lurking around us at all times ready to strike at a moment's notice. Neither should we believe that they can easily overpower us. They can't, because God doesn't let them.

We cannot avoid the temptations of the world, the flesh, and the devil, but these are indirect influences of the forces of evil, for which the Church has plenty of wholesome spiritual advice. In the same General Audience cited above, Pope John Paul II said: "We may think of the numerous exhortations to vigilance (cf. Mt 26:41; 1 Pet 5:8), to prayer and fasting (cf. Mt 17:21)." In other words, God has given us all the tools we need to avoid the indirect advances of the unholy ones into our lives.

We can add another basic point of common sense to this teaching. Generally speaking, we have much more to fear from the evil deeds of human beings than any direct harm from demons. That's because we cannot avoid associating with human beings, but we can – and must – avoid any direct association with demons. *They cannot harm us without our consent.* There is good reason for the Church's "No Contact Policy" I spoke of in Chapter 3.

One final thought about demons. If it's hard to get your mind around how ice angels can co-exist with the fires of hell, think of what we mean when we use the term "freezer burn".

Appendix 2

THE NINE CHOIRS OF ANGELS

FIRST HIERARCHY: THE REALM OF HEAVEN

Order	St. Thomas Aquinas[1]	Iconography	Scripture
Seraphim Hebrew: Saraph = "to burn", "burning ones"	Spiritual perfection: Charity. Fire moves upwards and continuously; heat; clarity. Superabundant fervor in leading others to God. Inextinguishable light.	Iconography: Pictured as red, with six wings; fire.	Is 6:1-7; seraph serpents with "burning" bite (cf. Num 21:6-9)
Cherubim Hebrew: Qerubim = "fullness of knowledge", "outpouring of wisdom"	Spiritual perfection: "Fullness of knowledge"; perfect vision of God; full reception of Light; contemplate beauty of divine order; overflow to others.	Iconography: Pictured as blue; four wings; four faces: man-ox-lion-eagle; eyes all over (peacock tail); fiery wheels.	Gen 3:24; Sir 49:8; Pss 17:11, 80:2, 99:1; Is 37:16; Ez chs. 1 and 10; Dan 3:55; Rev 4-7, 14-15, 19 Cherubim on the Ark of the Covenant: Ex 25:18-22; 1 Sam 4:4; 2 Sam 6:2; 1 Kgs 6:23-35; 2 Chr 3:7,10-14
Thrones Greek: θρόνοι Hebrew: Ophanim = "wheels"	Spiritual perfection: Strength, firmness, immovability; receive God in themselves and bear Him to others; openness to receive God; God accomplishes His judgments through them; they know immediately the things of God.	Iconography: Pictured as throne, mirror, seated on globe or throne or among celestial spheres.	Dan 7:9, Col 1:16

1. Aquinas, *Summa Theologica*, I.108.

The Nine Choirs of Angels 141

SECOND HIERARCHY: THE REALM OF THE UNIVERSE

Order	St. Thomas Aquinas	Iconography	Scripture
Dominions Greek: κυριότητες Latin: Dominationes [Dominions may also be called Dominations] Hebrew: Hashmallim	Spiritual perfection: Rigid and inflexible supremacy; these "illustrious heavenly princes" have the name of "lord" by participation because through them the inferior angels receive the divine gifts and are subject to them; participation in God's lordship; "appoint and order what belongs to the divine ministrations" (I.108.6).	Iconography: Pictured as weighing souls; carrying leader's staff; wielding orbs of light from staff or weapon.	Eph 1:21; Col 1:16
Virtues Greek: δυνάμεις Latin: Virtutes [Virtues are sometimes, but rarely, called Potencies or Strongholds]	Spiritual perfection: Excellence of strength; undertake fearlessly the divine behests appointed to them; power over corporeal nature in the working of miracles; participation in God's virtue; they give power for carrying out what is to be done.	Iconography: Pictured as miracle-working; act of piercing the devil.	Rom 8:38; 1 Cor 15:24; Eph 1:21; 1 Pt 3:22
Powers Greek: ἐξουσίαι Latin: Potestates [Powers are sometimes referred to as Authorities]	Spiritual perfection: Impose order on those subject to them; coerce evil spirits; participation in God's true dominion; determine how the divine decrees can be carried out by others.	Iconography: Pictured as dressed in armor; in act of chaining devil.	[Dan 3:61;] 1 Cor 15:24; Eph 1:21; Eph 3:10; Eph 6:11; Col 1:16; Col 2:10; Col 2:15; 1 Pt 3:22

Third Hierarchy: THE REALM OF THE WORLD AND MEN

Order	St. Thomas Aquinas	Iconography	Scripture
Principalities Greek: ἀρχαί Latin: Principatus [Principalities may also, but rarely, be called Princedoms or Rulers]	<u>Spiritual perfection</u>: Presidency; first in the execution of divine judgments; they preside over other angels in the execution of God's will.	<u>Iconography</u>: Pictured as armed with a shield, sword, or spear; wearing crown and holding scepter.	Rom 8:38; 1 Cor 15:24; Eph 1:21; Eph 3:10; Eph 6:11; Col 1:16; Col 2:10; Col 2:15; Jud 1:6 "Angels who kept not their principality but forsook their habitation."
Archangels Greek: ἀρχάγγελοι Latin: Archangeli Hebrew: rav-malakh "chief messenger"	<u>Spiritual perfection</u>: They announce to men great things above reason; the highest messengers or chief ambassadors.	<u>Iconography</u>: Michael dominant; escorts souls ("M. row your boat ashore"); pictured as holding scrolls; Gabriel: blowing trumpet! Virgin Mary; Raphael: healing, fish, Tobias, dog.	Tobit; Dan 8-12; Lk 1:10-20, 26-38; 1 Thes 4:16; Jud 1:9
Angels Greek: ἄγγελοι Latin: Angeli Hebrew: malakhim	<u>Spiritual perfection</u>: They announce God's will to men; They are messengers.	<u>Iconography</u>: Pictured with wings; guardians; helpers.	"Virtually every page of scripture speaks of angels" (St. Gregory the Great).

Appendix 3

PRAYER FOR AN ANGELIC HEART

Father of all angelic spirits and lofty origin of everything that exists, open my heart to a deep awareness of that glorious spirit of holiness who watches over me during every moment of my existence, my dear guardian angel.

I know by faith that he is present to me even when I am not aware of him, that he faithfully executes your will on my behalf even when I wander aimlessly through this world. Yet, I would know him more perceptively and love him more keenly.

I wish to pay attention to his sweet voice with fullest concentration and to see the workings of his immensely humble power all around me because he is the very whisper of your voice, the effective realization of your will that moves the world and influences the affairs of men.

I beg that you might take from me all manner of illusory thinking and self-seeking that inhibits my perception of this totally selfless being. Give me an angelic heart to know him and to love him, and in so doing, to love you more deeply every day.

Expand my soul to become a vessel of such openness that I might be filled with the immense riches of your Heart that are conveyed by his hand to my soul with such abundance. Let his goodness overflow from me to others in constant streams of grace.

Above all, allow me to have a discerning heart, like Solomon of old, to know the depth, height, breadth, and length of your love that comes to me through the ministry of my beloved angel.

And when I am one day allowed to meet him face-to-face in the Kingdom of Heaven, and enter into my eternal rest, may I finally be his faithful and constant companion in the holy mission, working side-by-side with him to bring the rest of humanity into your home forever.

I ask this through the intercession of the Queen of Angels, the ever-holy Virgin Mary, Mother of God, in the Name of Jesus Christ, our Lord.

Amen.

BIBLIOGRAPHY

Mortimer J. Adler, *The Angels and Us*, NY: MacMillan Publishing Company, Inc., 1982.

Charlene Altemose, MSC, *What You Should Know About Angels*, Liguori, Missouri: Liguori Publications, 1989.

Joan Wester Anderson, *An Angel to Watch Over Me: True Stories of Children's Encounters with Angels*, Chicago: Loyola Press, 2012.

_____, *Angels and Wonders: True Stories of Heaven on Earth*, Chicago: Loyola Press, 2008.

_____, *Guardian Angels: True Stories of Answered Prayers*, Chicago: Loyola Press, 2006.

_____, *In the Arms of Angels: True Stories of Heavenly Guardians*, Chicago: Loyola Press, 2004.

_____, *Where Angels Walk: True Stories of Heavenly Visitors*, NY: Ballantine Books, 1993.

Mike Aquilina, *Angels of God: The Bible, the Church, and the Heavenly Hosts*, Cincinnati, Ohio: Servant Books, 2009.

St. Thomas Aquinas, *Summa Theologica*, translated by the Fathers of the English Dominican Province, Benziger Bros. edition, 1947. I, QQ. 50-64 (Treatise on Angels) and 107-114 (Treatise on the Divine Government).

_____, *The Homilies of St. Thomas Aquinas*, tr. John M. Ashley, BCL, Ft. Collins, Colorado: Roman Catholic Books, n.d.

Benedict Ashley, O.P., ed., *Thomas Aquinas: The Gift of the Spirit*, Hyde Park, NY: New City Press, 1995.

David E. Aune, *Apocalypticism, Prophecy and Magic in Early Christianity: Collected Essays*, Tübingen, Germany: Mohr Siebeck, 2006.

William Barclay, The Daily Study Bible Series, *The Revelation of John, Vols. 1 &2*, Edinburgh, Scotland: The Saint Andrew Press, 1976.

G. K. Beale, The New International Greek Testament Commentary, *The Book of Revelation: a Commentary on the Greek Text*, Grand Rapids, Michigan: William B. Eerdmans Publishing Co., 1999.

James Stuart Bell, *Angels, Miracles, and Heavenly Encounters: Real-life Stories of Supernatural Events*, Minneapolis, Minnesota: Bethany House Publications, 2012.

Stephen Bemrose, *Dante's Angelic Intelligences: Their Importance in the Cosmos and in Pre-Christian Religion*, Roma, Italia: Edizioni di Storia e Letteratura, 1983.

Pope Benedict XVI, *Address to Artists*, Sistine Chapel, Vatican City, Europe, 2009.

Ladislaus Boros, *Angels and Men*, tr. John Maxwell, NY: The Seabury Press, 1976.

F. J. Boudreaux, S. J., *The Happiness of Heaven: And How to Attain the Joys That Await You There*, Manchester, New Hampshire: Sophia Institute Press, 1999.

Ian Boxall, Black's New Testament Commentary, *The Revelation of St. John*, Peabody, Massachusetts: Hendrickson Publishers, 2006.

Raymond Brown, et al. (eds.), *The Jerome Biblical Commentary*, Englewood Cliffs, New Jersey: Prentice-Hall, Inc., 1968.

Matthew Bunson, *The Angelic Doctor: The Life and World of St. Thomas Aquinas*, Huntington, Indiana: Our Sunday Visitor Inc., 1994.

Charles and Annette Capps, *Angels*, Tulsa, Oklahoma: Harrison House, 1984.

Catechism of the Catholic Church, Città del Vaticano: Libreria Editrice Vaticana, 1994.

Adela Yarbro Collins, *Crisis and Catharsis: The Power of the Apocalypse*, Philadelphia: The Westminster Press, 1984.

Compendium to the Catechism of the Catholic Church, Città del Vaticano: Libreria Editrice Vaticana, 2006.

Janice T. Connell, *Angel Power*, NY: Ballantine Books, 1995.

Joan Carroll Cruz, *Angels and Devils*, Rockford, Illinois: TAN Books and Publishers, 1999.

Jean Danielou, S.J., Christian Classics Series, tr. David Heimann, *The Angels and Their Mission*, Notre Dame, Indiana: Ave Maria Press, 1957.

Anthony DeStefano, *Angels All Around Us: A Sightseeing Guide to the Invisible World*, NY: Image, 2011.

Evaristus Eshiowu, *The Latin Mass* Magazine, "The Forgotten Army," Spring 2000.

John Farina, ed., The Classics of Western Spirituality Series, *Pseudo Dionysius: The Complete Works*, NY: Paulist Press, 1987.

Austin Farrer, *The Revelation of St. John the Divine*, Oxford, England: Oxford University Press, 1964.

Mary Ann Fatula, *Thomas Aquinas: Preacher and Friend*, Collegeville, Minnesota: The Liturgical Press, 1993.

H.M. Féret, *The Apocalypse Explained*, Fort Collins, Colorado: Roman Catholic Books, 1958.

Robert J. Fox, *The World and Work of the Holy Angels*, Alexandria, South Dakota: Fatima Family Apostolate, 2001.

Meredith J. Gill, *Angels and the Order of Heaven in Medieval and Renaissance Italy*, NY: Cambridge University Press, 2014.

Bob Glaze, *Angels: A Historical and Prophetic Study*, Oklahoma City, Oklahoma: Hearthstone Publishing, Ltd., 1998.

Malcolm Godwin, *Angels: An Endangered Species*, NY: Simon and Schuster, 1990.

Billy Graham, *Angels: God's Secret Agents*, Dallas, Texas: Word Publishing, 1994.

Jack Graham, *Angels: Who They Are, What They Do, and Why It Matters*, Bloomington, Minnesota: Bethany House, 2017.

Thomas H. Green, S.J., *Weeds Among The Wheat, Discernment: Where Prayer and Action Meet*, Notre Dame, Indiana: Ave Maria Press, 1986.

Scott Hahn, *The Lamb's Supper: The Mass as Heaven on Earth*, NY: Doubleday, 1999.

John A. Hardon, S.J., *Catholic Catechism on the Angels*, Bardstown, Kentucky: Eternal Life, 2000.

_____, *Meditations on the Angels*, Bardstown, Kentucky: Eternal Life, 2006.

Fr. John Horgan, *His Angels at Our Side: Understanding Their Power in Our Souls and the World*, Irondale, Alabama: EWTN Publishing, Inc., 2018.

Georges Huber, *My Angel Will Go Before You*, Dublin, Ireland: Four Courts Press, 2006.

David Jeremiah, *Angels: Who They Are and How They Help, What the Bible Reveals*, Colorado Springs, Colorado: Multnomah Books, 1982.

Pope John Paul II, *Letter to Artists*, Città del Vaticano: Libreria Editrice Vaticana, 1999.

Timothy Jones, *Celebration of Angels*, Nashville, Tennessee: Thomas Nelson Publishers, 1994.

Charles Journet, et al., *Le Péché De L'Ange: Peccabilité, Nature et Surnature*, Paris: Beauchesne et Ses Fils, 1961.

Howard P. Kainz, *"Active and Passive Potency" in Thomistic Angelology*, Bloomington, Indiana: iUniverse, 2012.

David Keck, *Angels and Angelology in the Middle Ages*, NY: Oxford University Press, 1998.

St. M. Faustina Kowalska, *Divine Mercy in My Soul: The Diary*, Stockbridge, Massachusetts: Marian Press, 2001.

Peter Kreeft, *Angels (and Demons): What Do We Really Know About Them?* San Francisco: Ignatius Press, 1995.

_____ (ed.), *Summa of the Summa*, San Francisco: Ignatius Press, 1990.

Judith Lang, *The Angels of God: Understanding the Bible*, NY: New City Press, 1997.

René Laurentin, *El Demonio ¿Símbolo o Realidad?* Bilbao, España: Desclée De Brouwer, 1995.

Bob and Penny Lord, *Heavenly Army of Angels*, Journeys of Faith: n.p., 1992.

Jacques Maritain, *The Sin of the Angel: An Essay on a Re-Interpretation of Some Thomistic Positions*, tr. William S. Rossner, S.J., Westminster, Maryland: The Newman Press, 1959.

Alfred McBride, O. Praem., *The Second Coming of Jesus: Meditation and Commentary on the Book of Revelation*, Huntington, Indiana: Our Sunday Visitor, Inc., 1993.

Bernard McGinn, ed., et al. Classics of Western Spirituality Series. *Angelic Spirituality: Medieval Perspectives on the Ways of Angels*, Mahwah, New Jersey: Paulist Press, 2002.

Ralph McInerney, *St. Thomas Aquinas*, Notre Dame, Indiana: University of Notre Dame Press, 1982.

Megan McKenna, *Angels Unawares*, Maryknoll, NY: Orbis Books, 1995.

J. B. Midgley, CTS Companions, *Companion to the Angels*, London, England: The Incorporated Catholic Truth Society, 2000.

Joel J. Miller, *Lifted By Angels: The Presence and Power of Our Heavenly Guides and Guardians*, Nashville, Tennessee: Thomas Nelson, Inc., 2012.

Mark Miravalle, "Angels Explained: What You Should Know About the Nine Choirs", Lighthouse Catholic Media Audio CD, 2013.

_____, *Time to Meet the Angels: The Nine Choirs and Much More*, Homer Glen, Illinois: Gabriel Press, 2013.

Daphne D.C. Pochin Mould, *Angels of God: Their Rightful Place in the Modern World*, NY: The Devin-Adair Company, 1963.

Robert H. Mounce, The New International Commentary on the New Testament, *The Book of Revelation*, Grand Rapids, Michigan: William B. Eerdmans Publishing Co., 1977.

Amy Newmark, *Touched By an Angel: 101 Miraculous Stories of Faith, Divine Intervention, and Answered Prayers*, Cos Cob, Connecticut: Chicken Soup for the Soul Publishing, LLC, 2014.

Irene Nowell, OSB, *101 Questions & Answers on Angels and Devils*, Mahwah, New Jersey: Paulist Press, 2010.

Catherine Odell and Margaret Savitskas, *Angels of the Lord: 365 Reflections on Our Heavenly Guardians*, Huntington, Indiana: Our Sunday Visitor, Inc., 2016.

Robert Leo Odom, *Israel's Angels Extraordinary*, Bronx, NY: Israelite Heritage Institute, 1985.

Opus Sanctorum Angelorum website: www.opusangelorum.org

Fr. Paul O'Sullivan, O.P., *All About the Angels*, Rockford, Illinois: TAN Publishers, 1990.

Elaine Pagels, *Revelations: Visions, Prophecy, and Politics in the Book of Revelation*, NY: Viking Penguin, 2012.

Fr. Alessio Parente, OFM, Cap., *"Send Me Your Guardian Angel": Padre Pio*, Foggia, Italia: Editions "Carlo Tozza Napoli-Dicembre 1984," n.d.

Pascal P. Parente, *The Angels: The Catholic Teaching of the Angels*, Rockford, Illinois: TAN Books, 1994.

Eric Peterson, *The Angels and the Liturgy*, NY: Herder and Herder, 1964.

Guillermo Pons, *Los Angeles en Los Padres de la Iglesia*, Madrid: Ciudad Nueva, 2003.

Jessica Powers, *The Selected Poetry of Jessica Powers*, Regina Siegfried and Robert Morneau, eds., Kansas City, Missouri: Sheed and Ward, 1989.

Ron Rhodes, *The Secret Life of Angels: Who They Are and How They Help Us*, Eugene, Oregon: Harvest House Publishers, 2008.

Albert Joseph Mary Shamon, *Apocalypse: The Book For Our Times*, Milford, Ohio: The Riehle Foundation, 1999.

Giovanni Siena, *Padre Pio: This is the Hour of the Angels*, tr. Julie L. Mitchell, n.p., 1997.

Stephen S. Smalley, *The Revelation to John: A Commentary on the Greek Text of the Apocalypse*, Downers Grove, Illinois: InterVarsity Press, 2005.

St. Michael and the Angels, Rockford, Illinois: TAN Books and Publishers, 2008.

Perry Stone, *This Season of Angels: Angelic Assignments During This Prophetic Season*, FaithWords, 2018.

Francisco Suárez, S.J., *De Angelis*, Lib. i-iv, vii, tr. Sydney Penner, PDF, 2009.

Andrew Sulavik, Knights of Columbus Veritas Series, *All About Angels*, Catholic Information Service: New Haven, Connecticut, 1999.

Adolphe Tanqueray, S.S., D.D., *The Spiritual Life: A Treatise on Ascetical and Mystical Theology*, Charlotte, North Carolina: TAN Books (An Imprint of St. Benedict Press, LLC), 2000.

Marianne Lorraine Trouvé, FSP, *Angels: Help from on High*, Boston, Massachusetts: Pauline Books and Media, 2010.

Mark Twain, *Personal Recollections of Joan of Arc*, San Francisco: Ignatius Press, 1989.

James C. Vanderkam, *The Dead Sea Scrolls Today*, Grand Rapids, Michigan: William B. Eerdmans Publishing Co., 1994.

Juan Martin Velasco et al., *Angeles y Demonios*, Madrid, España: Fundación Santa María, 1984.

Claus Westermann, *God's Angels Need No Wings*, tr. David L. Scheidt, Philadelphia: Fortress Press, 1979.

Jane Williams, *Angels*, Grand Rapids, Michigan: Baker Books, 2007.

T.J. Wray and Gregory Mobley, *The Birth of Satan: Tracing the Devil's Biblical Roots*, NY: Palgrave MacMillan, 2005.

ACKNOWLEDGMENTS

It is impossible to express my depth of gratitude to John Collins, my selfless friend and mentor, for his constant help in honing the writing craft. He's been with me since day one in the multi-year process of bringing this book to fruition. He is an invaluable source of wisdom and support.

I'd also like to thank Gene Van Son, my editor at the Catholic Stand, for his painstaking attention to my manuscript and his lightning fast responses and patience with my deficits. His insightful contributions truly strengthened and augmented this work.

The professional talents of Barbara Rose and Steve Kuhn have given this book its final, beautiful form, and I am extremely grateful for their service.

Finally, I cannot fail to thank Sr. Patricia Marie Barnette, RGS, who is a long-time friend, spiritual ally, and source of support. She has a whole community of nuns praying for me. It's the kind of assistance one cannot buy in this world.

ABOUT THE AUTHOR

Peter Darcy is a writer and editor who spent thirty years in the non-profit sector and various business enterprises. His great passion is educating others about the power of Beauty, Truth, and Goodness. In 2020 he launched the *Sacred Windows* initiative for this purpose.

Natures of Fire is his tenth book.

Visit *Sacred Windows* at www.sacredwindows.com
and his author's website at www.peterdarcywriting.com.

GET THE COMPANION EDITION TO THIS BOOK

Natures of Fire Study Guide

Available now at Strength of Soul Books

www.strengthofsoulbooks.com

publisher@strengthofsoulbooks.com

ALSO BY PETER DARCY

*Mister Buddy's Guide to Non-Profit Leadership:
Principles for Success in a Charitable World*
(Tremendous Leadership, 2019)

The Seven Leadership Virtues of Joan of Arc
(Tremendous Leadership, 2020)

*No-Nonsense Non-Profit: Leadership
Principles for Church and Charity
(Strength* of Soul Books, 2020)

AMDG